# JOSEPH

## Also by Bill Crowder

Before Christmas

For This He Came

God of Surprise

Gospel on the Mountains

King Solomon

Let's Talk

My Hope Is in You

One Thing Is Necessary

Overcoming Life's Challenges

Seeing the Heart of Christ

The Spotlight of Faith

Windows on Christmas

Windows on Easter

Wisdom for Our Worries

### Devotionals

A Compassionate Heart

A Present Peace

# JOSEPH

## CULTIVATING A LIFE OF DEPENDENCE ON GOD

## BILL CROWDER

Our Daily Bread
Publishing.

*Joseph: Cultivating a Life of Dependence on God*
© 2025 by William Crowder

Interior design by Michael J. Williams

**Library of Congress Cataloging-in-Publication Data Available**

*Printed in the United States of America*
25  26  27  28  29  30  31  32  /  8  7  6  5  4  3  2  1

For
my editor and friend
Joel Armstrong.
It's a privilege working together!

*There is meaning in every journey that is unknown to the traveler.*

Attributed to Dietrich Bonhoeffer

# CONTENTS

# ACKNOWLEDGMENTS

For years I did not fully appreciate the value of character studies in the Bible. I was more comfortable doing verse-by-verse exposition with a theological focus. And that is certainly important. However, I was then exposed to some of the writings of G. Campbell Morgan, who would become my favorite Bible teacher (though he was long dead when I discovered him). This was followed up by reading books by Bible teachers such as Gene Getz, Donald Campbell, and Chuck Swindoll—all of whom have done extensive work with Bible characters. I was beginning to see the light.

The value of learning the practical lessons from the lives of Bible characters came to full bloom when I started doing international Bible conferences for RBC Ministries (now Our Daily Bread Ministries). The first conference I did was on Jonah, and it went swimmingly (pun intended). The next was an exposition of the little New Testament letter from Jude. It is filled with riddles, puzzles, and solid doctrinal truth. The responses to those two series could not have been more diverse. I learned that many people struggle with abstract concepts—even sound theological ones. But encase those concepts in a person's story and people identify with them much more quickly.

Obviously, this book is a character study born from that journey in ministry and teaching. So, I want to begin by acknowledging those influences who helped steer me in a very positive direction. I also want to once again express my gratitude to Don Hescott, who opened the door for me to first speak at Bible conferences in the United States, and Albert Lee, who made possible the same teaching platform internationally. Thirty years later, these stories still reach into people's hearts and make a difference.

I also want to express my ongoing gratitude for Chriscynethia Floyd, Dawn Anderson, and the team at Our Daily Bread Publishing for their continued trust and help in producing these volumes. A special thank-you is due to my editor Joel Armstrong, without whose brilliant editing this book would have never made it into your hands.

My wife, Marlene, and her faithful, steadying support are absolutely invaluable, and she has heard these messages more than anyone else (perhaps more than anyone should!). Yet she still believes in the value and power of the biblical story of Joseph and has not grown the least bit numb to its strength and value.

# INTRODUCTION
## *Life Is Tough*

Aside from our Lord Himself, Joseph (the Old Testament one) is my all-time favorite Bible character. In fact, I have taught a Bible conference series on Joseph some thirty times domestically in the United States and around the world. And it will come as little to no surprise that his story has resonated with the broadest cross section of people imaginable. His story connects with people everywhere regardless of age, gender, nationality, ethnicity, culture, or career.

Joseph is a timeless character, and the struggles he faced are absolutely relevant to our generation. Seeing his reliance on God in those struggles can encourage our trust in God as well. Perhaps most notably, Joseph shares with us the common human experience of broken relationships. Do you know that feeling? You walk into a room, and someone gets up and walks out. They won't respond to your phone calls, texts, or emails. When you try to talk to them, they just turn and walk away. A broken relationship is one of the most painful things in life.

But it is not the only difficult challenge we face in this broken world. Betrayal or misrepresentation by others, being forgotten by people we have tried to help, and impossibly difficult life situations can either break us profoundly or become the instruments God uses to build us to a strength we never imagined possible.

As we examine Joseph's story together, may our God give us the wisdom and courage to become travelers on this journey who are fueled by trust in the God who already knows all the unknown struggles we will face. We can learn from Joseph's example. So, join me in exploring a truly outstanding person who did that hard work of trusting God—and his God used him quite literally to change his world.

# 1

# A FAMILY IN DYSFUNCTION

## GENESIS 37:1-4

How do you enter the world? By that, I don't mean how you were born. I mean, How do you engage life? Process life? Understand life?

A friend of mine enters the world through nature. For him, everything makes more sense when viewed through the lens of God's majestic creation. One of my sons enters the world through numbers, so he spends pretty much every working hour staring at screens filled with spreadsheets that are likewise filled with numbers. For him, that is how life makes sense.

So, how do *you* enter the world?

For me, I enter the world through music. In fact, there are a lot of things in the world I wouldn't know about had I not heard a song about it. One example is "Stone of Sisyphus" by the band Chicago. When I heard the song, I became curious. I had never before heard of Sisyphus and wanted to know what he was all about.

The song is rooted in a story from ancient Greece. Sisyphus, a mythological king of Corinth, offended the gods so severely that Zeus condemned him to an eternity of pushing a boulder up the side of a mountain. Every time he reached the zenith of the mountain, Sisyphus would watch helplessly as the boulder came crashing back down to the bottom of the mountain—from

15

whence Sisyphus had to start over. For all eternity. In Homer's ancient *Odyssey*, the hero, Odysseus, descends into Hades and observes Sisyphus's torment, describing it this way:

> Then I witnessed the torture of Sisyphus, as he wrestled with a huge rock with both hands. Bracing himself and thrusting with hands and feet he pushed the boulder uphill to the top. But every time, as he was about to send it toppling over the crest, its sheer weight turned it back, and once again towards the plain the pitiless rock rolled down. So once more he had to wrestle with the thing and push it up, while the sweat poured from his limbs and the dust rose high above his head.[1]

What a phenomenal metaphor for life in a fallen, broken world. And while it may feel descriptive of many of our experiences, it absolutely describes Joseph's life. Just when it seemed he was making some progress, just when it seemed he was getting somewhere, just when it seemed he was getting ahead, the boulder of life would roll back down the mountain and he would have to start over. And over. And over. Starting with his terribly dysfunctional family.

## Dysfunction 101

Our kids were all still young and at home when the term *dysfunctional family* entered our consciousness. Our quick-witted offspring liked to joke to their friends, "Our family puts the fun in dysfunctional." While funny and clever, the truth is that there is nothing humorous about families in dysfunction.

What makes a family dysfunctional? According to Mental Health America,

A dysfunctional family is characterized by "conflict, misbehavior, or abuse." Relationships between family members are tense and can be filled with neglect, yelling, and screaming. You might feel forced to happily accept negative treatment.

There's no open space to express your thoughts and feelings freely. You aren't able to thrive and feel safe within your own family . . . And that's just the tip of the iceberg.

No family acts the same—and all families experience some level of dysfunction. But there are some clear signs you can look for to indicate bigger problems.

These problems include addiction, perfectionism, abuse or neglect, unpredictability and fear, conditional love, lack of boundaries, lack of intimacy, and poor communication.[2]

**When we drill down into Joseph's family history, we see generations of abuse of the marriage relationship, which inevitably poisoned the sibling relationships in the children and grandchildren of those marriages.**

As a pastor, I found myself occasionally dealing with families in dysfunction, and it created a deep sense of frustration because the people involved often could not recognize the characteristics of dysfunction that seemed fairly obvious to outside observers. The dysfunction had become so embedded in their family life that, for them, these things seemed normal.

Inevitably, the seedbed for dysfunction in a family is dysfunction in the marriage. No family is stronger or healthier than the husband-wife relationship upon which it is built. Neglect and anger in the marriage always find their way to the parent-child and sibling relationships as well. When we drill down into Joseph's family history, we see generations of abuse of the marriage relationship, which inevitably poisoned the sibling relationships in the children and grandchildren of those marriages with poor communication, conditional love, and fear.

*Abraham (Joseph's great-grandfather):* God had promised a son to Abraham—a son through whom all the world would be blessed. When it began to seem that God had forgotten that promise, Abraham joined the plan of his wife, Sarah, to produce a son differently: Abraham slept with and impregnated Sarah's handmaiden Hagar. When she bore the son that Sarah conspired to create, the friction levels in the household grew to disastrous levels, causing Hagar and Ishmael (her son by Abraham) to be banished from the camp (Genesis 16).

When God kept His promise and Sarah gave birth (in her extreme old age!) to Isaac, the jealousy and conflict between Sarah and Hagar became unbearable (Genesis 21). This animosity was transferred to Abraham's two sons (Galatians 4:28–29), and it continues even to today in the conflict between Israel (the descendants of Isaac) and the surrounding nations (the descendants of Ishmael). All because of sibling tensions rooted in one child being favored over the other.

*Isaac (Joseph's grandfather):* The only patriarch who appears to have had an unspoiled marriage, Isaac nevertheless repeated the failure of favoritism he received from his father, Abraham. Having two sons, Esau and Jacob, Isaac favored Esau while his wife, Rebekah, favored Jacob (Genesis 27). This dual favoritism resulted in such friction between the brothers that Jacob (who contributed greatly to the conflict) was forced to leave the country for safety with distant relatives.

*Jacob (Joseph's father):* The patriarch Jacob (renamed Israel), son of Isaac and grandson of Abraham, fled for his life to where his relatives were. There, he began building his family when he acquired not one but two wives. He then compounded the problem by not only having children by both of them but also having children by their handmaidens, Bilhah and Zilpah. The result was that he had twelve sons—but only two of those sons were by the wife he truly loved, Rachel. Joseph and his younger brother, Benjamin, the sons of Rachel, were given the status of most favored, with Joseph in the chief position.

This was not a minor thing. In their culture, being the son who inherited was everything. He would then have headship of the family and ownership of everything. So, when Joseph was so obviously loved more by Jacob, the brothers reacted with hate—no doubt feeling threatened by Jacob's preference and love for Joseph.

This background may seem like it's just unnecessarily dragging skeletons out of closets, but it isn't. Seeing the family history is necessary if we are to appreciate the steps that took Joseph from his most-favored status in Canaan to the position of a slave in Egypt (which will be the focus of chapter 2). Throughout the history of this family was a pattern of sibling rivalry—Isaac versus Ishmael, Jacob versus Esau, Joseph versus everybody—usually fueled by unwise parenting or flawed marriage relationships. This heritage of sibling rivalry even traced back to the first two siblings—Cain and Abel—and I suspect we are all aware of the tragic outcome of that broken relationship (Genesis 4).

## Misguided Favoritism (Genesis 37:1–4)

> Now Jacob lived in the land where his father had lived as a stranger, in the land of Canaan. These are the records of the generations of Jacob.
>
> Joseph, when he was seventeen years of age, was pasturing the flock with his brothers, while

he was still a youth, along with the sons of Bilhah and the sons of Zilpah, his father's wives. And Joseph brought back a bad report about them to their father. Now Israel loved Joseph more than all his other sons, because he was the son of his old age; and he made him a multicolored tunic. And his brothers saw that their father loved him more than all his brothers; and so they hated him and could not speak to him on friendly terms.

Jacob's misguided favoritism of Joseph was obvious to all in the family, and Joseph and Benjamin became outcasts in their own family by becoming their father's favorites. Clearly, Joseph exacerbated this situation when he ratted out his half brothers (v. 2)—expanding even further the distance the brothers perceived between themselves and their dad. Remember, Joseph was seventeen years old. In his immaturity, no doubt trying to please his father, Joseph might as well have walked into a room filled with dynamite carrying a blazing torch! He would need to grow beyond that immaturity.

> **Jacob's choice to ignore God's principles (both in marriage and in his parenting) and his lack of wisdom would tear his family apart.**

Jacob's choice to ignore God's principles (both in marriage and in his parenting) and his lack of wisdom would tear his family apart—shredding it down to its basic fibers. How? By awarding Joseph with a special coat, there was now an outward symbol of his favoritism. Some scholars say that "a multicolored tunic" (v. 3) could be translated as "a coat with sleeves." If so, then not only did the coat signal Joseph's favored status, it also may have signaled that he was not expected to work to the same level as his brothers. Sleeves would be an encumbrance to the physical work so common in the ancient world. So, to have a coat with sleeves would have excused Joseph from the physical labor expected of the other brothers. This special coat will become a key element of the story going forward.

The result? Notice again Genesis 37:4:

> His brothers saw that their father loved him more than all his brothers; and so they hated him and could not speak to him on friendly terms.

The heart of the problem is their father, Jacob. The brothers saw the definitive evidence of his love for Joseph—apparently to the exclusion of his loving them—and, because they couldn't hate their father, they turned their hate on Joseph. Additionally, the narrator adds that they "could not speak to him [Joseph] on friendly terms." I encourage you to file that thought away for later in the story.

For now, the condition in Jacob's family reveals to us several problems:

- The atmosphere of conflict and tension between the siblings is rooted in problems in Jacob's marriage relationships. Jacob's polygamy is the heart of the problem (see 1 Samuel 1 for a similar example), for the obvious and inevitable competition between the wives translated into tension and ill will between the children as well. By the way, polygamy isn't required for this to occur. The husband-wife relationship is still the primary and critical relationship in the home and sets the temperature for all the other relationships. A marriage that is filled with tension will convey that tension through the relationships with and between the children.

- The ignorance of Jacob in showing preference to one son over the others carries a heartbreaking price tag—not only because of the twisted signals it sends the favored child but also because of the pain of rejection experienced by the unpreferred.

- The lack of fairness undermines the integrity of the family and the credibility of the parents. When my own children were growing up, there were often times when we allowed one of the older kids to do something the younger kids were disallowed from. Once or twice, the younger came to me and protested rather vigorously, "Why did you let them do that? You wouldn't let me!" To that I responded, "Because I love them more." To that the offended child responded, "No, you don't!" To which I could say, "Okay, then, let's have a conversation without all the accusations," and we worked it out from there. As long as the child felt fairly loved, circumstances could be navigated.

We have already seen that all families have a certain amount of dysfunction, simply due to our fallenness. I grew up in a family of seven kids, having three brothers and three sisters. I am thankful that, in the midst of the uncertainties a large family can bring, there was never any doubt about Mom and Dad's love for each other. Their devotion to each other was absolute—giving our family a strong and solid base on which to build and grow.

Nevertheless, among the boys—especially the three of us who were older—there was tremendous competition for our parents' attention. My brothers were amazing athletes, with two of my brothers going to college on baseball scholarships and my other brother becoming a state handball champion.

In my case, athletically I was a late bloomer. It wasn't until college that I began to have any success in sports—and that was in soccer, a sport my parents neither understood nor cared about. Since I couldn't compete in the realm of athletics, I focused on academics, with membership in the National Junior Honor Society and National Honor Society as my main achievements. For a lot of kids growing up, they dread the day their parents have to sign their report cards. Not me. That was always one of my happiest days because I knew Mom and Dad would be pleased with my grades.

Now understand, my parents loved us all and treated us all with great care. But competition between brothers is a natural thing. Our competition was often superheated—not because our parents demanded it but because we wanted to show them what we could do. When sibling rivalry is so naturally rooted in us, it doesn't take much to get that proverbial ball rolling. Now, these many years later, we brothers have grown into good friends—but still with a competitive edge that comes out whenever we play golf together. But even at their very worst, our competitions were tame and toothless compared to what Joseph experienced with his brothers.

Joseph lives in a family filled with strife, deception, and self-interest. The seedbed of this tension? The poor parenting practices of Jacob himself. His actions, rather than stemming the tide of family anger, exacerbated it. The result? Hate! Jacob's lack of wisdom and discernment, combined with his bad parenting choices, watered his household with gasoline—and Joseph is about to strike a match!

## Home as a Breeding Ground

What is bred in your home? The home can be a breeding ground for either the most profound kind of love or the most severe and intense hate. What are you building? What have you built?

Years ago, I came across a piece called Donohoe's will, dated July 1, 1935. This actually was quoted in an *Our Daily Bread* article from 1994. Listen to the depth of pain and resentment that a dysfunctional family can produce, as Donohoe renders his estate to his two daughters:

> Unto my two daughters, Frances Marie and Denise Victoria, by reason of their unfilial attitude toward a doting father, . . . I leave the sum of $1.00 to each and a father's curse. May their lives be fraught with misery, unhappiness, and poignant sorrow. May their deaths be soon and of a lingering malignant and torturous nature. . . . May their souls rest in hell and suffer the torments of the condemned for eternity.[3]

How tragic! While this represents the extreme, causing us to think, "Wow, maybe my family isn't so bad after all!" it should also jar us into taking a long look at our families. What do we as individuals contribute to the health or brokenness of our family and its various relationships? Rather than casually assuming our family isn't so bad, perhaps we could ask instead, "How can I contribute to making my family healthier and stronger? How can I be a force for love and understanding when tensions arise?"

You could even pray that the Lord grows in you the fruit of the Spirit, so that those aspects of a healthy heart can be an influence for good and for God within your family. Paul wrote to the churches of Galatia:

> But the fruit of the Spirit is love, joy, peace, patience, kindness, goodness, faithfulness, gentleness, self-control; against such things there is no law. (Galatians 5:22–23)

"Against such things there is no law" is such a wonderfully encouraging reality! There is no place, no situation, no relationship that isn't strengthened by the infusion of these spiritual fruit. That just might be the best place to start seeking healing and strengthening for your family—even if it's a dysfunctional one.

And beyond our earthly families, we also have a family of faith, made up of Christ followers from around the world. Yes, that family is not perfect either, but the head of that family is Christ Himself. And He is perfect! So, in the midst of our imperfect, sometimes dysfunctional earthly families, we have a heavenly family that we will celebrate with forever. In an old hymn, John Fawcett wrote of the ideal heart of a church family, and what an ideal it is:

> Blest be the tie that binds
> Our hearts in Christian love;
> The fellowship of kindred minds
> Is like to that above.
>
> From sorrow, toil, and pain,
> And sin, we shall be free;
> And perfect love and friendship reign
> Through all eternity.

## Questions for Personal Reflection or Group Discussion

1. All families have their own particular problems. What are the primary struggles in your family? Do they rise to the level of dysfunction as defined in this chapter?
2. How could Jacob have more wisely handled his relationships in his home? Given his plural marriages and resulting multiple children, his case is not normal, but we can still learn from his failings.

25

3. How could Joseph have more wisely handled his relationships with his brothers? How was (or is) tattling handled in your family?

4. Can you identify with the brothers' resentment of Joseph? Why or why not? Why was their resentment misdirected?

5. How can you apply the fruit of the Spirit to conflict in your family?

# 2

# AN ACT OF TREACHERY

## GENESIS 37:5-36

My all-time favorite quote comes from a volume called *The Cynic's Quotebook*. It declares, "The dream that all men should live as brothers is held by men who have no brothers." As I have already stated, I have three brothers, as well as three brothers-in-law, so I understand the tension and frustration addressed in this quote. Brothers can fight like cats and dogs yet defend each other to the last breath. Relationships between brothers have a rather complex dynamic—as we have already seen in the brother relationships in the book of Genesis.

This dynamic also contributed to America's Civil War (also known as the War between the States)—a war that often pitted brother against brother. At its core, the Civil War was not about land or wealth; it was about two distinctly different value systems determining what society should look like, and many times brothers found themselves on opposite sides of that equation. Families were often divided over the issue of slavery—with part of the family being committed abolitionists and part of the family pushing for the states to decide the issue rather than a central federal government. There were many incidents of brothers fighting against brothers:

- William Rufus Terrill, a general in the Union Army, was killed at the Battle of Perryville on October 8, 1862. *Encyclopedia Virginia* adds, "Two of Terrill's brothers, James and Philip, were killed fighting for the Confederacy. According to legend, their father placed a monument to his slain sons that read, 'This monument erected by their father. God alone knows which was right.'"[1]
- On November 7, 1861, Union Navy Commander Percival Drayton "commanded a ship in the Port Royal expedition, in which Union forces captured Hilton Head Island, Beaufort, and Parris Island in order to gain a base for operations against Savannah and Charleston. In the battle his brother Thomas, a Confederate brigadier general, commanded the forts whose guns exchanged fire with Drayton's ship."[2]
- James and Alexander Campbell, born in Scotland, "found themselves fighting each other for their adoptive countries at Secessionville in 1862. . . . The Charleston Courier editorialized on the two brothers, 'another illustration of the deplorable consequences of this fratricidal war.' It stated Alexander Campbell, 'fought gallantly in the late action' and 'displayed . . . a heroism worthy of his regiment and a better cause' while James Campbell 'was conspicuous and has been honorable mentioned on our side.'"[3]

These and countless other brother-versus-brother incidents occurred during the War between the States, and many had tragic outcomes. However, not all brother-versus-brother scenarios play out on such a grand scale. Sometimes the friction between brothers occurs because of a momentary flash point. At other times, it is the product of an extended period of time where perceived injustice or unkindness leads to deeper emotions. Over time, even without heated political arguments feeding the flames, bitterness can accumulate in the hearts of people and become regretfully destructive.

This kind of intense bitterness was what led to Joseph being sold into slavery—by his own brothers.

## Joseph's Immaturity (Genesis 37:5–16)

I have often heard or read that Joseph was a type of Christ. A *type* is an Old Testament representation that anticipated a New Testament reality. But was Joseph such a type? One writer thought so, saying, "While only Jesus was truly sinless, Joseph is one of the few people significantly written about in the Bible of which no sins are mentioned."[4] While I admit that Joseph in many ways led an exemplary life, he nonetheless displayed failures—especially in his relationships with his brothers.

Some might not class these failings as sins per se, but at the very least they were highly damaging failures that hurt others and exacerbated the rising tide of tensions in Jacob's family. The root of these failings? An immaturity fed by his father's displays of favoritism that led Joseph to be a bit self-absorbed and insensitive to the feelings of those around him. Though the major contributing factor to the family's dysfunction was Jacob's poor parenting and multiple marriages, Joseph's insensitivity and lack of discernment only increased the friction levels in this badly broken family to an explosive level. Notice Genesis 37:5–11:

> Then Joseph had a dream, and when he told it to his brothers, they hated him even more. He said to

**Joseph's insensitivity and lack of discernment only increased the friction levels in this badly broken family.**

them, "Please listen to this dream which I have had; for behold, we were binding sheaves in the field, and behold, my sheaf stood up and also remained standing; and behold, your sheaves gathered around and bowed down to my sheaf." Then his brothers said to him, "Are you actually going to reign over us? Or are you really going to rule over us?" So they hated him even more for his dreams and for his words.

Then he had yet another dream, and informed his brothers of it, and said, "Behold, I have had yet another dream; and behold, the sun and the moon, and eleven stars were bowing down to me." He also told it to his father as well as to his brothers; and his father rebuked him and said to him, "What is this dream that you have had? Am I and your mother and your brothers actually going to come to bow down to the ground before you?" His brothers were jealous of him, but his father kept the matter in mind.

Perhaps passing on the first dream to his brothers was nothing more than youthful exuberance—after all, Joseph was only seventeen years old. But coming back with the second dream shows a lack of concern for how the first dream had impacted his brothers. Verse 5 pulls no punches in candidly relating the events:

Joseph had the first dream.
Joseph told the dream to his brothers.
His brothers hated him even more for it.

In ancient times, dreams were often seen as messages from God (or in pagan cultures, the gods). As such, from the perspective of the brothers, it's as if Joseph is rubbing salt into their wounds. It isn't enough that he is their father's favorite; now he is declaring himself to be God's favorite as well! The imagery of the dream—his sheaf of grain standing upright and theirs bowing to him—was undeniably clear to the brothers, as they respond, "Are you actually going to reign over us? Or are you really going to rule over us?" (v. 8).

Remember that ancient tradition saw the leadership of the family pass to the oldest son—but Joseph was almost the youngest. But there is something else here—a nuance that would be easy to miss if we weren't paying attention. Notice the end of verse 8, "So they hated him even more for his dreams and for his words." It wasn't just the content of the dream that so thoroughly agitated the brothers; it was also his *words*. There was something about the way he told them the dream. Something in his voice or tone or speech conveyed a spirit that nearly set fire to this combustible situation.

All of that tension seems to have flown right past Joseph for, upon having a second dream, he tells that one to them as well. Almost as if he were saying, "That went so well the first time, I can't wait for them to hear this one!" But this time the dream expanded to include his parents bowing before him. Jacob scolded Joseph for so casually and callously lording this dream over his brothers and family—but Jacob also "kept the matter in mind" (v. 11).

As the tension continues to build, Joseph shows his lack of character, for he lacks discretion and discernment. He lacks interest and insight into the hearts and needs of those around him—what we today call emotional intelligence. While Jacob did not display these qualities in his relationship with his own brother Esau, neither does Joseph with his brothers. Joseph has received the promise of future leadership, but he abuses that leadership. While it is true that one day he *will* exercise dominion over them, he clearly isn't ready for it yet. His flaunting of the promise makes that obvious. Joseph must learn that to be a leader, you must first become a servant. One of the greatest necessities at any level of leadership is to realize the servanthood of leadership—and that is where Joseph's weaknesses are exposed. This glaring deficiency in Joseph's young life, however, will be addressed in the slave pits of Egypt, where he will learn how to serve the hard way.

How does this come about? In our first introduction to Joseph, he is bringing to his father a "bad report" about his brothers (v. 2). What was the nature of that report? We are not told, but it can't have gone down well with the brothers. When I was a kid, we called that being a tattletale. Tattletales were not easily overlooked or forgiven because the unspoken assumption was that the motive for their tattling was to gain advantage. In a family, tattling is often an attempt to gain the parent's approval at the expense of the sibling or siblings. To the one tattled on, it feels like a gross violation of trust. Joseph's past tattling sets the stage for what's next in Genesis 37:12–16:

> Then his brothers went to pasture their father's flock in Shechem. And Israel said to Joseph, "Are your brothers not pasturing the flock in Shechem? Come, and I will send you to them." And he said to him, "I will go." Then he said to him, "Go now and see about the welfare of your brothers and the welfare of the flock, and bring word back to me." So he sent him from the Valley of Hebron, and he came to Shechem.
>
> A man found him, and behold, he was wandering in the field; and the man asked him, "What are you looking for?" He said, "I am looking for my brothers; please tell me where they are pasturing the flock."

Is it hard to believe that Jacob may have sent Joseph to check on his brothers in hopes of getting another bad report? It isn't hard for me to believe that, given Jacob's character and history. So off Joseph goes searching for his brothers, and when he can't find them, a stranger gives directions to where they had gone. It is there that a life-changing—eventually even a world-changing—confrontation takes place.

## The Brothers' Ferocity (Genesis 37:17–28)

Have you ever experienced the true, deep-seated, shocking rage of another person? As a very young pastor, I remember being in a monthly board meeting. We were discussing some matter of church business that has long since drifted into the fog of memory, when suddenly one of the board members—a genteel, wise, elderly man with brilliant white hair—leaned across the table and started screaming at me. Between his threatening to punch me and daring me to punch him, it was easily the most uncomfortable meeting I've ever attended. When finally he caught his breath and stormed out of the meeting, I just stared at the other men with my mouth hanging open. They seemed as stunned by what had transpired as I was.

As uncomfortable as that meeting was, there is rage and then there is RAGE. Growing up in West Virginia, from my early days I heard of the historic Appalachian feud between the Hatfields and the McCoys. This feud raged in southern West Virginia from 1863 to 1891 and resulted in between twelve and twenty people being murdered. The feud "attracted nationwide attention . . . and prompted judicial and police actions, one of which drew an appeal up to the U.S. Supreme Court (1888)."[5]

So, when you think of rage, think Hatfields versus McCoys—and overlay that imagery on Genesis 37 to get a sense of the rage the brothers felt for Joseph.

Then the man said, "They have moved from here; for I heard them say, 'Let's go to Dothan.'" So Joseph went after his brothers and found them at Dothan.

When they saw him from a distance, and before he came closer to them, they plotted against him to put him to death. They said to one another, "Here comes this dreamer! Now then, come and let's kill him, and throw him into one of the pits; and we will say, 'A vicious animal devoured him.' Then we will see what will become of his dreams!" But Reuben heard this and rescued him out of their hands by saying, "Let's not take his life." Then Reuben said to them, "Shed no blood. Throw him into this pit that is in the wilderness, but do not lay a hand on him"—so that later he might rescue him out of their hands, to return him to his father. So it came about, when Joseph reached his brothers, that they stripped Joseph of his tunic, the multicolored tunic that was on him; and they took him and threw him into the pit. Now the pit was empty, without any water in it.

Then they sat down to eat a meal. But as they raised their eyes and looked, behold, a caravan of Ishmaelites was coming from Gilead, with their camels carrying labdanum resin, balsam, and myrrh, on their way to bring them down to Egypt. And Judah said to his brothers, "What profit is it for us to kill our brother and cover up his blood? Come, and let's sell him to the Ishmaelites and not lay our hands on him, for he is our brother, our own flesh." And his brothers listened to him. Then some Midianite traders passed by, so they pulled him up and lifted Joseph out of the pit, and sold him to the Ishmaelites for twenty shekels of silver. So they brought Joseph into Egypt. (vv. 17–28)

Yes, indeed: the dream that all men should live as brothers is held by men who have no brothers.

Notice how quickly the situation escalates. First, Joseph's brothers see him coming at a distance. How did they know it was him? No doubt because of his one-of-a-kind coat—the symbol of his favored status with their father. Then, when they speak of Joseph, they do so with sarcasm, which fairly drips from the words "this dreamer" (v. 19). But, not content to merely insult Joseph behind his back, they strategize a way to be rid of him. Perhaps they feel that, with Joseph gone, the love of their father will come to them. Their plan has no subtlety, just a savage hatred that seeks to destroy the object of their hate—their own brother. And even that proposal carries bitter sarcasm: "Let's kill him, and throw him into one of the pits; and we will say, 'A vicious animal devoured him.' Then we will see what will become of his dreams!" (v. 20).

His dreams are so great! How are they going to work out if we kill him? This scheme begins to form in their minds but is soon trumped by Reuben—the oldest and, by culture, the brother with the most to lose to Joseph in terms of potential inheritance. Reuben urges them not to kill Joseph but rather to drop him into a nearby pit, intending to come back and rescue him later. So, upon Joseph's arrival, they strip him of his special coat, which symbolizes everything they hate about Joseph, and cast him into the pit without food or water.

Undoubtedly Joseph is in shock. He no sooner arrives at his brothers' location after a wearying search when he is pounced upon by his own kin. Confused and a bit sore, he languishes in the pit for some time. I'm convinced he spent that time wondering what he had done to make them respond that way to him. But while he is in the pit, the brothers—led by Judah (more on him later)—concoct a new plan. Rather than kill Joseph, they decide to sell him to Ishmaelite traders (remember the conflict between Isaac and Ishmael?) who are traveling to Egypt, where he can be sold into slavery. Why kill Joseph when there is potential profit to be made by selling him?

Their rage has apparently become cold-blooded, as they plot their brother's destruction while they sit down to enjoy a meal (v. 25). As Joseph struggles in the pit, they lounge and relax. That is some heartlessness. It reminds me of the soldiers who crucified our Lord. As He hung on the cross, the soldiers were "sitting down" and "began to keep watch over Him there" (Matthew 27:36), almost as if they were enjoying the show of Jesus's suffering. That same coldheartedness is seen here in Joseph's brothers.

Why is Judah at the front of this effort to remove Joseph from their family? Oddly enough, the name Judah means "praise" or "thanksgiving," yet he seems to have taken on his father's mantle of schemer and conniver rather than that of a praiser. His pushing the group to sell Joseph into slavery will be countered later in the story by a brilliant moment of sacrifice that will be shocking in its own right.

But, for now, Judah is scheming. Why? Some scholars believe that because his three older brothers had been disqualified from the inheritance because of sin (Genesis 34; 35:22), his position had risen as the fourth-born son. If so, Judah is now the one who has everything to gain by Joseph's disappearance—but at what cost would that advantage be gained?

## The Resulting Heartache (Genesis 37:29–35)

> Now Reuben returned to the pit, and behold, Joseph was not in the pit; so he tore his garments.

He returned to his brothers and said, "The boy is not there; as for me, where am I to go?" So they took Joseph's tunic, and slaughtered a male goat, and dipped the tunic in the blood; and they sent the multicolored tunic and brought it to their father and said, "We found this; please examine it to see whether it is your son's tunic or not." Then he examined it and said, "It is my son's tunic. A vicious animal has devoured him; Joseph has surely been torn to pieces!" So Jacob tore his clothes, and put on a sackcloth undergarment over his waist, and mourned for his son many days. Then all his sons and all his daughters got up to comfort him, but he refused to be comforted. And he said, "Surely I will go down to Sheol in mourning for my son." So his father wept for him.

What are the results of all this tension, anger, and hatred? This is an important question to ask, because we don't always stop to think about the results ahead of time—but inevitably they come anyway. See what comes of this:

- Reuben mourns for Joseph (and his own lack of courage). As the oldest brother, he felt a sense of responsibility for Joseph's welfare.
- The brothers lie to their father but never escape their personal guilt (see 42:22). I can imagine the scene as they hand their father Joseph's bloodstained one-of-a-kind coat. "Do you recognize this? It seems oddly familiar to us." "It is Joseph's!"
- Jacob, the deceiver, is now deceived, with a pain and mourning that refuse to be comforted. Jacob reaps what he

has sown. He deceived his father, Isaac, with the blood of a goat (Genesis 27), and now his sons do the same to him in a classic illustration of the law of sowing and reaping (Galatians 6:7).

• If the brothers hoped for Joseph's absence to open the door for them to receive Jacob's love, they are disappointed. Jacob is inconsolable and refuses to be comforted.

Joseph had reached the top of the family mountain. He had his father's love, the special coat, the preferential treatment. But like Sisyphus, Joseph sees the boulder roll all the way down the mountain, and he must start over. In Egypt. As a slave. But, in spite of the tragic results, God will take the brothers' evil in Joseph's life and bring good out of it. With hindsight that is twenty-twenty, Joseph himself will declare that reality in Genesis 50:20:

> In spite of the tragic results, God will take the brothers' evil in Joseph's life and bring good out of it.

As for you, you meant evil against me, but God meant it for good in order to bring about this present result, to keep many people alive.

### Individual Responses (Genesis 37:36)

Meanwhile, the Midianites sold him in Egypt to Potiphar, Pharaoh's officer, the captain of the bodyguard.

Where are we? Back in Canaan, Jacob and the brothers are suffering for their sins, but Joseph is learning to trust God with the outcomes of life—even when those outcomes are woven with the dark threads of treachery. Joseph has now arrived in Egypt, where God will take those dark threads and use them to make Joseph effective as a man and a leader.

What are the dark threads in your life? Like Joseph, we must learn to trust God with them, for we should never be afraid to trust the God we know with a future that is unknown.

F. R. Havergal wrote in her beautiful hymn what that confident trust in God looks like:

> Take my life and let it be
> Consecrated, Lord, to thee.
> Take my moments and my days;
> Let them flow in endless praise,
> Let them flow in endless praise.
>
> Take my will and make it thine;
> It shall be no longer mine.
> Take my heart it is thine own;
> It shall be thy royal throne,
> It shall be thy royal throne.

## Questions for Personal Reflection or Group Discussion

1. What difficult experiences might God be repurposing for good in your life?

2. Looking back at the painful disappointments in your life, how might God have been sparing you—protecting you from something worse than just disappointment?

3. Think of a painful relationship in your past. How might you have handled it more wisely?

4. Now flip the script. Who is someone you may have hurt or disappointed? Have you ever apologized or sought their forgiveness? If not, will you?

5. Why is it so hard to trust God with our dark threads? When have you been able to remain confident of His love and good purposes even in hard times?

# 3

# THE LIFE OF A SLAVE

## GENESIS 39:1-6

Arguably the most beloved of all Christian hymns, "Amazing Grace" has an interesting background. John Newton, the author of the song, spent many years of his life as the captain of a slaving ship. Later, in 1748, Newton became a believer in Christ, a minister of the gospel, and a staunch abolitionist. Clearly, when he penned the phrase "that saved a wretch like me," he wasn't expressing false humility. He saw his years in the slave trade as a nightmare that haunted him. Celebrating God's grace in the face of what he had been forgiven was a necessary and proper response from Newton's heart.

Some years ago, my wife, Marlene, and I visited Liverpool, England, where I was teaching for a Bible conference. On a day off, we visited the touristy area of Albert Dock, flush against the River Mersey. Among the coffee shops and souvenir stands were several museums: The Beatles Story, the Maritime Museum, and the International Slavery Museum. It is fitting that Liverpool is the home of the slavery museum because Liverpool was the third point of the slave trade triangle. Ships departed from Liverpool—a major port city—for West Africa, where they picked up their human cargo and proceeded to the Caribbean Islands, where the slaves were put to work in the sugar fields. Then the ships carried their load of sugar back to England.

Throughout Liverpool are reminders of the slave trade, as many of the streets, like Penny Lane, are named for wealthy people who earned their wealth off of slavery. But the museum itself is worth a long, thoughtful visit. There is an immersive audiovisual experience of what it was like for the slaves in transit on the slave ships. It is an emotionally devastating experience, as are many of the exhibits.

The result of the visit for me, aside from a renewed sense of the horrific inhumanity that is slavery, was an awakened appreciation for those like Newton, William Wilberforce, Olaudah Equiano, Ignatius Sancho, Mary Prince, and others who fought for decades to eradicate the slave trade. Among them was a Christian scholar who was an expert in New Testament Greek. This scholar, Granville Sharp, said, "A toleration of slavery is, in effect, a toleration of inhumanity." That quote is literally carved in stone at the entrance of the museum—and it is still true today, for we live in a world that is rife with slavery, often referred to as human trafficking.

For those of us in the West, our understanding of slavery is shaped by the way it was practiced in colonial times and early America. Slavery in the Bible, however, was qualitatively different from that in early America. Slavery in America was race-based, with the slave trade importing laborers from West Africa as the slave trade triangle operated, but in the Bible it was not. In fact, in ancient cultures people could sell themselves into slavery (as bondslaves) if they felt it was the way they could best provide for themselves and their family (see Exodus 21:2–11).

This brings us back to Joseph. When we left him in the previous chapter, he had been sold into slavery by his brothers. Exploring Joseph's life as a slave is both painful and necessary if we are to understand how he rose, by God's grace, to a position of trust and responsibility in Potiphar's house.

Dr. Mark Janzen, a professor of archaeology and ancient history, describes what slavery in ancient Egypt was like:

> Slaves plowed fields, planted and harvested crops, tended cattle, and worked with textiles in service to temple estates. They could also serve as butlers, beer-makers, fan-bearers, shield-bearers, and mercenaries. An Egyptian official, Setau, used foreign slaves to construct and work at the temple at the Wadi es-Sebua. Slaves were also brick-makers, as depicted in a famous scene from the tomb of the vizier Rekmire (ca. 1450 B.C.E.) and in a leather scroll now housed in the Louvre dating to Ramesses II.
>
> At the workmen's village of Deir el Medina, the state provided slaves for individual households; these slaves were paid in grain rations and may even have been rented out to others, allowing the original owner to earn additional income from their labor. . . .
>
> Overall, slaves played many roles in New Kingdom Egypt, a highly complex society that came to increasingly rely on slave labor for its economic prosperity.[1]

But all of that speaks in generalities. In the specifics of Joseph's case, the anonymous author of Psalm 105 described his experience this way:

> He called down famine on the land
>     and destroyed all their supplies of food;
> and he sent a man before them—

Joseph, sold as a slave.
They bruised his feet with shackles,
  his neck was put in irons,
till what he foretold came to pass,
  till the word of the LORD proved him true.

(vv. 16–19 NIV)

The "he" in view is God Himself, who in preparation for the massive worldwide famine to come later in Genesis "sent a man before them—Joseph, sold as a slave." The Scriptures are sparse in describing what that experience included, but it is fairly easy to imagine the challenges involved.

At age seventeen, he is sold into slavery by his brothers and taken to Egypt—a foreign land. Presumably, the first task before the young man was learning the language. How could he ever perform his tasks if he didn't understand what he was told to do or the expectations of how to accomplish that task? Think of the time involved just in that process.

Second, as Jacob's favorite son, whose special coat may have implied that he was exempted from work, Joseph probably was a bit soft and pampered. He needed to toughen up and develop his physical strength in order to do whatever forced labor was thrown his way. In the midst of those experiences, Joseph's exuberance of emotion, as expressed in his telling his dreams to his brothers—twice—would need to grow into a maturity that could control his emotions, especially when receiving ill treatment from Egyptian taskmasters. Remember what Moses witnessed in Exodus 2:11:

One day, after Moses had grown up, he went out
to where his own people were and watched them
at their hard labor. He saw an Egyptian beating a
Hebrew, one of his own people. (NIV)

Beating was not only used as a punishment for failed tasks or inadequate performance of those tasks; it was also used to control the slaves. Responding to such harsh treatment would have required a mature, cool head—one that, to this point in the story, Joseph has not exhibited.

All of these learning and growing experiences would follow what had to have been a severe case of shock and disorientation when Joseph first arrived in Egypt. Taken together, all of this points to the fact that Joseph had a lot of growing up to do if he was to survive this most unwanted of experiences.

## Joseph's Landing Spot (Genesis 39:1)

> Now Joseph had been taken down to Egypt; and
> Potiphar, an Egyptian officer of Pharaoh, the captain
> of the bodyguard, bought him from the Ishmaelites,
> who had taken him down there.

On its surface, Joseph's situation doesn't seem particularly imposing, but further investigation shows otherwise. There is some debate among scholars as to Potiphar's role as one of Pharaoh's officials. The phrase "captain of the bodyguard" has been understood in different ways.

- As the English words imply, some see this role as the head of Pharaoh's protective crew—not unlike the director of the United States Secret Service, who protects the American president and other top officials.
- Others define the role as chief warden of the royal prison.
- Still others interpret the role as chief executioner.

Color me crazy, but as unpleasant and daunting as being sold into slavery would be, finding that you had become the property of the chief executioner would magnify the intensity of your new life status exponentially. How terrifying! Joseph is a teenager, now the property of one of Pharaoh's top officials, and alone in a foreign country.

But is that so? Is Joseph really alone?

### A Long Season of Learning (Genesis 39:2–3)

> And the LORD was with Joseph, so he became a successful man. And he was in the house of his master, the Egyptian. (v. 2)

Joseph had been abandoned by his family, but he had not been abandoned by his God! The Lord was with Joseph. Did that make slavery easy or pleasant? Probably not, but it did make it endurable.

With the Lord's help, Joseph applied himself to the work and the challenges of that work:

> Now his master saw that the LORD was with him and that the LORD made all that he did prosper in his hand. (v. 3)

Don't pass over that verse too quickly. Sit with it for a moment and consider a couple of things. It is likely that Joseph spent ten years serving Potiphar after arriving in Egypt. Ten years of slavery, mistreatment, hard labor, and deprivation. Ten years of isolation from family and home. Ten years. (We'll see later how we arrive at such a number.)

> **Joseph had been abandoned by his family, but he had not been abandoned by his God!**

Take a moment and think of where you were and what you were doing ten years ago. Periodically my Facebook algorithm will show me a memory of something I posted years ago. Occasionally I will smile and think to myself, *I remember that. That was a good day.* Or sometimes I will reflect on a largely difficult moment. Either way, ten years is a long time. Much happens in those years. Much is forgotten. Life changes.

For Joseph, much more than just "much" has changed. He has transformed from a spoiled kid into a robust man—and that man has earned his master's trust.

> The character qualities of a God-honoring leader that were absent in Genesis 37 now start to become visible in Joseph's life.

### Joseph's Growing Status (Genesis 39:4–6)

> So Joseph found favor in his sight and became his personal servant; and he made him overseer over his house, and put him in charge of all that he owned. It came about that from the time he made him overseer in his house and over all that he owned, the LORD blessed the Egyptian's house on account of Joseph; so the LORD's blessing was upon all that he owned, in the house and in the field. So he left Joseph in charge of everything that he owned; and with him there he did not concern himself with anything except the food which he ate.

Imagine how painful it must have been at age seventeen not only to be sold into slavery and torn from your family—but to have your family be the agents of that sale. It would have been so easy to become embittered and filled with hate (like his brothers), but Joseph didn't. He reacted rightly to the hardness of the situation, and as a result the character qualities of a God-honoring leader that were absent in Genesis 37 now start to become visible in Joseph's life. In a sense, Joseph will become the prototype of a Psalm 1 man, all because of the presence of the Lord.

The presence of the Lord is a marvelous reality to live in. It was what set Joseph apart, even against his personal skills, which were indeed considerable. The whole chapter of Genesis 39 stresses God's presence with Joseph (vv. 2, 3, 21, 23) and the effect that presence had on Potiphar. He could not help but recognize the presence of God in Joseph's life.

How real is God's presence to you? To me? Can anyone else see that presence in our lives? Imagine the caliber of Joseph's testimony that Potiphar, a thoroughgoing pagan, not only saw the difference and admired the difference—but attributed it not to Joseph but to the God of the Hebrews (v. 3)!

Apparently Joseph was not bitter about his brothers or enslaved by his circumstances—but instead was content with the presence of God. It's a great thought, isn't it? The New Testament encourages us to this kind of contentment as well:

> Make sure that your character is free from the love of money, being content with what you have; for He Himself has said, "I will never desert you, nor will I ever abandon you," so that we confidently say,

> "The Lord is my helper, I will not be afraid. What will man do to me?"
> (Hebrews 13:5–6)

> But I rejoiced in the Lord greatly, that now at last you have revived your concern for me; indeed, you were concerned before, but you lacked an opportunity to act. Not that I speak from need, for I have learned to be content in whatever circumstances I am. (Philippians 4:10–11)

Joseph doesn't mourn his disappointment but is determined to become useful where he is. And God blesses that heart of faithfulness and contentment, as the one faithful in a few things is raised to a position of stewardship over greater things.

Potiphar recognizes God's hand on Joseph, coupled with the young man's skills and character, and makes Joseph his household manager. He places Joseph over his entire household—supervising other servants and employees, handling public relations, overseeing finances, administering agricultural and business interests. Joseph is even responsible for the provisions for all of Potiphar's household.

It seems that everything Joseph touches is blessed. Now, perhaps ten years after being sold into slavery, Joseph is on top of the world. But, two things must be seen:

1. His success is not because of Joseph, but rather due to the presence of God.
2. Now, in success and prosperity, Joseph is most vulnerable to trial and temptation.

My all-time favorite hymn captures the wonder and beauty of living in God's presence. The sixth-century Irish poet Dallán Forgaill wrote those words from his heart, and they speak to mine every time I sing or hear them:

> Be Thou my vision, O Lord of my heart.
> Naught be all else to me, save that Thou art.
> Thou my best thought, by day or by night;
> Waking or sleeping, Thy presence my light.
>
> Be Thou my wisdom, and Thou my true word;
> I ever with Thee and Thou with me, Lord;
> Thou my great Father, and I Thy true son,
> Thou in me dwelling and I with Thee one.

"Thy presence my light. . . . I ever with Thee and Thou with me, Lord." What a wonderful assurance! God's presence can be the most real reality we ever experience, for He is there—whether we acknowledge His presence or not.

## Questions for Personal Reflection or Group Discussion

1. When have you experienced a long season of struggle? What was that like?

2. What lessons did you take away from that difficult season? How might those lessons have prepared you for your current season of life?

3. How conscious are you of God's presence in your life?

4. What are some practical ways you could practice or be more aware of God's presence in your life?

5. How can awareness of God's presence help in difficult times?

# 4

# BETRAYED AGAIN

## GENESIS 39:6–23

As I mentioned in the previous chapter, one of my favorite places to visit is Liverpool, England. I grew up on the Beatles and am now a passionate supporter of Liverpool Football Club (long stories on both counts). When I think of Liverpool, I think of places like Strawberry Field, Penny Lane, and Royal Albert Dock, home of The Beatles Story museum.

But I also think of the International Slavery Museum when I think of Liverpool. And when I think of the slave trade in England, I think of two people—William Wilberforce and his pastor, John Newton (1725–1807). Yes, again, the John Newton who wrote "Amazing Grace." I have often felt that, had it been written when Joseph was alive, the third verse could have been the soundtrack for Joseph's life.

> Through many dangers, toils and snares
> I have already come:
> 'Tis grace has brought us safe thus far,
> And grace will lead me home.

Such was the life of Joseph. His life was filled with incredible highs and disheartening lows. Through both, the Lord was with Joseph (Genesis 39:2, 3, 21, 23). That reality is critically important because it explains the resilience we see in this young man. For perhaps ten years, Joseph had been climbing his way out of the pit of slavery, and at long last he achieved something. He reached the status of Potiphar's household manager. For a slave, that was about as good as it got. The years of shackles (Psalm 105:17–18) and backbreaking labor seemed to be behind him as he reached a "white-collar" position in Potiphar's household.

This should be a wonderful moment of relief and satisfaction, but remember the mythological story of Sisyphus. When he got to the top of the mountain, the boulder would roll all the way to the bottom, and he had to start all over again. Now, once again, the stone is going to roll back down the mountain for Joseph by means of yet another act of treachery—and all because of something that should have been a good thing:

> Now Joseph was handsome in form and appearance. (v. 6)

The years of slave labor had turned the soft boy from Canaan into a robust and desirable man. Joseph was a good-looking guy and apparently pretty ripped from the years of hard labor. I must confess that I have never been overly attractive, but back in my high school and college days, I often thought what a blessing it was for those who were attractive. It seemed to make life that little bit easier when you're good-looking.

Then I studied the life of Joseph and realized that with that blessing came potential for problems. For Joseph, those problems came encapsulated in the person of Mrs. Potiphar—the original desperate housewife!

## When Blessings Turn Brutal (Genesis 39:7–12)

What follows is a fascinating study in sexual desire (on the part of Potiphar's wife) and spiritual commitment (on the part of Joseph). Each of them knows what they want from this situation. She wants a sexual conquest, and he wants to maintain his purity and integrity. And each has a strategy to achieve their personal goals.

> And it came about after these events that his master's wife had her eyes on Joseph, and she said, "Sleep with me." But he refused and said to his master's wife, "Look, with me here, my master does not concern himself with anything in the house, and he has put me in charge of all that he owns. There is no one greater in this house than I, and he has withheld nothing from me except you, because you are his wife. How then could I do this great evil, and sin against God?" Though she spoke to Joseph day after day, he did not listen to her to lie beside her or be with her. Now it happened one day that he went into the house to do his work, and none of the people of the household was there inside. So she grabbed him by his garment, saying, "Sleep with me!" But he left his garment in her hand and fled, and went outside.

Let's consider her strategy first.

She begins with a sort of flattery, perhaps seeking to appeal to Joseph's male ego. This flattery is found in her, the master's wife, offering herself to a slave, saying, "Sleep with me." (v. 7). Everything else in the household is under Joseph's control—why not her as well?

When that is unsuccessful, she implements her second plan of attack. She seeks to wear him down. In verse 10 she speaks

53

to him "day after day." Which could easily read "day after day after day after day after day." She is trying to wear him down by spiritual erosion, like dripping water wearing away a great rock over time. But that plan also fails.

For her final plan of action, she actually attacks Joseph and tries to drag him to her bed. If she is nothing else, she is relentless. When there was no one else in the house, "she grabbed him by his garment, saying, 'Sleep with me!'" (v. 12). This assault of an enslaved man was the equivalent of attempted rape—showing just how desperate this desperate housewife truly was.

So, we see her strategy:

1. Offering herself as a form of flattery.
2. Wearing Joseph down with erosive tactics.
3. Physically attacking him to force herself on him.

Wow. That is a lot to get our minds around, but it's also a reminder of how thoroughly evil an evil person can be. Her determination was to conquer Joseph sexually, but what she didn't realize was that Joseph also had a strategy to help him maintain purity. Joseph had a powerful set of convictions, and here's the fascinating thing about those convictions:

He didn't learn them from his father, Jacob.

He didn't learn them from his brothers.

He didn't learn them in pagan Egypt.

I believe these convictions represent the character produced by the ongoing presence of God in his life. That abiding presence produced a heart with strong convictions and a commitment to purity. And that purity and character battled the temptation.

Joseph's strategy for maintaining purity was learned in the

presence of the Lord who had faithfully been with him throughout his tragic story. The influence of God's presence on Joseph's heart, life, and value system was profound. And, while the actual methods of how that influence was achieved are not described for us, the reality of it is unavoidable when we consider Joseph's strategy.

When Mrs. Potiphar throws herself at him with flattery, Joseph responds by having the right concerns—both vertically and horizontally. Notice again Genesis 39:8–9:

> But he refused and said to his master's wife, "Look, with me here, my master does not concern himself with anything in the house, and he has put me in charge of all that he owns. There is no one greater in this house than I, and he has withheld nothing from me except you, because you are his wife. How then could I do this great evil, and sin against God?"

**Joseph's strategy for maintaining purity was learned in the presence of the Lord who had faithfully been with him throughout his tragic story.**

Joseph's horizontal concern is for his master, Potiphar. Can you hear him appealing to her for a sense of fair play? In a terrible, unwanted situation of slavery, Joseph has found favor with Potiphar and has received something very precious—Potiphar's trust. He says in essence, "He has put me in charge of everything. He trusts me! All that is withheld from me is you—because you are his wife. He trusts me, and I won't violate that trust for a one-night stand with you." His horizontal concern is for how such an act would hurt Potiphar.

His vertical concern is grounded in the reality of living in God's presence. "How then could I do this great evil, and sin against God?" (v. 9). It's as if he's saying, "God has helped me. Protected me. Faithfully cared for me. He has never abandoned me. How can I sin against Him like this with you? It would violate everything that is important to me in my relationship with my God."

That is a great starting place for a strategy for purity. But it doesn't end there. When Potiphar's wife tries to wear Joseph down, he applies part two of his strategy—avoidance. This is a strategy that is repeated elsewhere in Scripture:

> Therefore, treat the parts of your earthly body as dead to sexual immorality, impurity, passion, evil desire, and greed, which amounts to idolatry. (Colossians 3:5)

> For the lips of an adulteress drip honey,
> And her speech is smoother than oil;
> But in the end she is bitter as wormwood,
> Sharp as a two-edged sword.
> Her feet go down to death,
> Her steps take hold of Sheol.
> (Proverbs 5:3–5)

> For this is the will of God, your sanctification; that is, that you abstain from sexual immorality; that each of you know how to possess his own vessel in sanctification and honor, not in lustful passion, like the Gentiles who do not know God. (1 Thessalonians 4:3–5)

> All things are permitted for me, but not all things are of benefit. All things are permitted for me, but I will not be mastered by anything. Food is for the stomach and the stomach is for food, however God will do away with both of them. But the body is

not for sexual immorality, but for the Lord, and the Lord is for the body. (1 Corinthians 6:12–13)

Let's behave properly as in the day, not in carousing and drunkenness, not in sexual promiscuity and debauchery, not in strife and jealousy. But put on the Lord Jesus Christ, and make no provision for the flesh in regard to its lusts. (Romans 13:13–14)

That final verse provides a great summary of the second element of Joseph's strategy—alert avoidance.

While he has shown no interest in her, Mrs. Potiphar clearly does not like being told no. When she attacks Joseph physically, he applies part three of his strategy—he runs away (v. 12). What Samson, David, and Solomon failed to do, Joseph did. Joseph fled—but not as a coward. He fled as a man with the courage of his convictions and with his honor intact. As Paul told Timothy, "Now flee from youthful lusts and pursue righteousness, faith, love and peace with those who call on the Lord from a pure heart" (2 Timothy 2:22).

One word of caution here. As one old preacher said, "Don't flee from temptation only to wait around the corner for it to catch up!" The best way to deal with temptation is not to flirt with it, or argue with it, or reason with it. The best thing to do is flee from it! This is powerful stuff—Joseph resisted in spite of an evil environment, in spite of her persistence, and in spite of limited spiritual training. (Remember, this is four hundred years before the Mosaic law.) How?

He recognized that he belonged to God.

He recognized the effect of his sin on other people.

He recognized his sin as rebellion against God.

His character continues to be shaped and molded for young Joseph. Now, in a thirty-minute sitcom on TV, his commitment (if displayed at all) would have resulted in everyone living happily ever after. But real life doesn't always work that way. Life in a fallen world doesn't always reward people who do right. Joseph is about to learn an important life lesson—no good deed ever goes unpunished.

### When Doing Good Is Punished (Genesis 39:13–18)

> When she saw that he had left his garment in her hand and had fled outside, she called to the men of her household and said to them, "See, he has brought in a Hebrew to us to make fun of us; he came in to me to sleep with me, and I screamed. When he heard that I raised my voice and screamed, he left his garment beside me and fled and went outside." So she left his garment beside her until his master came home. Then she spoke to him with these words: "The Hebrew slave, whom you brought to us, came in to me to make fun of me; but when I raised my voice and screamed, he left his garment beside me and fled outside."

William Congreve wrote, and I paraphrase, that a certain nasty place hath no fury like a woman scorned—and this scorned woman has Joseph square in her sights. She calls the men of the household together and constructs a lie to get her revenge against Joseph for refusing her, using his outer garment (or coat) as alleged evidence of Joseph's wrongdoing. If you'll remember back to Genesis 37, this is now the second time an article of clothing has been used to lie about Joseph. If I were Joseph, I might just decide to never wear another coat for the rest of my life.

Having practiced her story on the men of the household, Mrs. Potiphar now tells her husband. How would he respond?

> Now when his master heard the words of his wife
> which she spoke to him, saying, "This is what your
> slave did to me," his anger burned. So Joseph's
> master took him and put him into the prison, the
> place where the king's prisoners were confined; and
> he was there in the prison. (39:19–20)

This is very, very interesting. Remember, Potiphar is one of Pharaoh's high officials—maybe the chief executioner. The point? He has options on how to deal with Joseph. Also, I am intrigued by the statement in verse 19 that "his anger burned." But at whom? At Joseph—or at his own wife? That's the question, isn't it?

The text doesn't explicitly define the direction of his anger, but it is not hard to imagine that, in fact, his anger is at her, not Joseph. He knows Joseph's character to the point that he has entrusted all he has to him. He also knows his wife, and it is not hard to imagine that this is not her first attempt at an extramarital dalliance.

So, the ball is in Potiphar's court. What will he do? His response, to me at least, shows that he knows his wife is lying, but he has to save face. Remember, Potiphar has options. In ancient Egypt, capital punishment "would normally have happened in rape cases."[1] The fact that Potiphar only has Joseph imprisoned says that he probably knew his wife was lying. At the very least, he knew this accusation was out of character for Joseph.

So Joseph ends up in prison—for doing the right thing! You might say, "But that's not fair!" And you'd be absolutely right. Life often is not fair. Listen to how this unjust result is described by the great Bible teacher Alexander Maclaren:

> So now we see him at the lowest ebb of his fortunes,
> flung down in a moment by a lie from the height

to which he had slowly been climbing, having lost the confidence of his master, and earned the unslumbering hatred of a wicked woman. He had wrecked his career by his goodness. "What a fool," says the world. "How badly managed things are in this life," say doubters, "that virtue should not be paid by prosperity!" But the end, even the nearer end of this life, will show whether he was a fool, and whether things are so badly arranged; and the lesson enforced by the picture of Joseph in the dungeon, and which young beginners in life have special need to learn, is that, come what will of it, right is right, and sin is sin, that consequences are never to deter from duty, and that it is better to have a clean conscience and be in prison than do wickedness and sit at a king's table. A very threadbare lesson, but needing to be often repeated.[2]

> **The mark of a life lived for God is a commitment to do what is right and pure—and to let God be concerned with the outcomes.**

The point? Life isn't fair—but that is not our concern. Our concern is to do what is right. The mark of a life lived for God is a commitment to do what is right and pure—and to let God be concerned with the outcomes.

Now, what of poor Joseph? He responded to slavery rightly, and he responded to success rightly. How will he respond to this?

### When God Is There (Genesis 39:21–23)

But the LORD was with Joseph and extended kindness to him, and gave him favor in the sight of the warden of the prison. The warden of the prison put Joseph in charge of all the prisoners who were in the prison; so that whatever was done there, he was responsible for it. The warden of the prison did not supervise anything under Joseph's authority, because the LORD was with him; and, the LORD made whatever he did prosper.

Joseph is unjustly imprisoned for doing the right thing—and the presence of God that was with him as he rose in Potiphar's house continues with him in prison. It is easy to ask, "Why be good, why do right, if you only end up here?" But, for Joseph, this prison is not his end. He has rested in the presence of God, and God has blessed him still with that presence.

Once again, Joseph begins to learn—and he is learning that the pains, problems, dangers, and trials of life all come into focus when we live in the reality of the presence of the sovereign God and trust His mercy. Joseph's is a character under construction:

Shaped by adversity
Punished by people
Honored by God

Remember that verse from "Amazing Grace" by John Newton? Once again, it beautifully captures Joseph's experience:

Through many dangers, toils and snares
I have already come:
'Tis grace has brought me safe thus far,
And grace will lead me home.

Joseph is not yet home, but God's grace and mercy are preparing the way. In the same way that the Lord was with him when he first arrived in Egypt and rose from despair to opportunity (vv. 2–3), so the Lord is with him as he is wrongly condemned to prison (vv. 21, 23). As he found favor with Potiphar, so now Joseph, by God's hand, finds favor with the warden of the prison.

We must never forget that our God is sovereign. He is in control, and we can rest in his control knowing that he makes no mistakes. To that point, the lesson here is simple: Joseph may be in prison unjustly, but he is not there by accident. God's continuing work will unfold in his life to bring about His good purposes for His young servant. And that we will see in the next chapters.

But at this point, had it been written, I wonder if Joseph might have hummed the words of H. G. Spafford's hymn while faithfully carrying out his responsibilities in prison:

> When peace, like a river, attendeth my way,
> When sorrows like sea billows roll;
> Whatever my lot, Thou hast taught me to say,
> It is well, it is well with my soul.
>
> It is well with my soul,
> It is well, it is well with my soul.

Whether we're rising or falling, it can be well with our soul if we trust our God and rest in His good purposes for us—in spite of the circumstances that may engulf us.

## Questions for Personal Reflection or Group Discussion

1. Have you ever encountered (or been) someone who plotted out and strategized for their sin? What were the elements of that strategy?

2. Joseph's strategy for maintaining purity showed a wisdom beyond his years. Do you agree that this wisdom was a

reflection of his living in God's presence? Why or why not?

3. In today's culture, what factors make maintaining purity so difficult?

4. How can you intentionally avoid cultural influences that could lead to impurity?

5. Spend a few moments in prayer asking God to help you to maintain purity in your life.

# 5

# FORGOTTEN AGAIN

## GENESIS 40

I'll confess, I'm not a huge flower guy—except when it comes to buying them for my beautiful wife. I know what a rose is and happily get them for Marlene whenever possible. Among the hundreds of other species of flowers that are lovely in their own right, I also know the beautiful forget-me-not. Often the flower consists of five rich blue petals stretching forth from a white center, making for a wonderful display. The forget-me-not typically blooms for a few weeks in April and May and is said to symbolize remembrance, true love, devotion, and royalty.

What intrigues me the most, however, is the name itself. Why are they called forget-me-nots? While there are several folktales about the flower's name, "in a German tale, when the Lord had finished naming all the plants, a small plant cried out 'Forget-Me-Not, O Lord!' He said, 'That shall be your name!'"[1]

All of us have experienced what it feels like to be forgotten—and it doesn't feel good. There have been times when, in a foreign country where English wasn't spoken, I was left at the airport by my driver and had to figure out how to get from there to the hotel. It happens. We are forgetful people, so sometimes we forget.

Young parents swamped with kids' schedules of soccer, baseball, gymnastics, dance lessons, piano lessons, and more can easily be overwhelmed and forget to pick up one of their children. But it is a decidedly different experience for the parent than it is for the child!

Years ago, when we lived in Southern California, I was watching a California Angels baseball game on TV when the color commentator, Joe Torre (who would later manage the New York Yankees to six American League titles and four World Series championships), said that he'd had an interesting experience upon arriving at the stadium for the game. As he waited for the elevator to the press box to call the game, a youngster came to him and asked, "Are you somebody?" Yes! He had been a Gold Glove–winning third baseman and a fearsome hitter during his career. He had been a nine-time all-star and the 1971 National League Most Valuable Player when playing for the St. Louis Cardinals. But, in that moment, none of those achievements were remembered.

And that brings us back to Joseph, who after helping a couple of strangers will be forgotten by them. But, because of his relationship with God, Joseph will be able to respond to disappointment with faithfulness and trust, showing that he is really learning the true patience that marks a person who has learned to "wait for the LORD" (Isaiah 40:31).

> **Because of his relationship with God, Joseph will be able to respond to disappointment with faithfulness and trust.**

The Lord is still with him as Joseph quietly goes about the business of faithfully serving in the jail where he has been falsely imprisoned. The lessons of leadership he has learned—faith, purity, commitment, sensitivity, a servant's heart—have prepared him for the next lesson, in which he must learn patience. That is the only proper response when we are faced with disappointment, particularly at the hands of other people. We must allow our hearts to be so anchored in our God that we are secure against disappointment.

What Joseph will learn is that, though he may be there unjustly, he is not there by accident.

## A Divine Appointment (Genesis 40:1–4)

> Then it came about after these things, that the cup-bearer and the baker for the king of Egypt offended their lord, the king of Egypt. And Pharaoh was furious with his two officials, the chief cupbearer and the chief baker. So he put them in confinement in the house of the captain of the bodyguard, in the prison, the same place where Joseph was imprisoned. And the captain of the bodyguard put Joseph in charge of them, and he took care of them; and they were in confinement for some time.

As we launch into Genesis 40, Joseph's situation has not changed. He is still in prison—unjustly—and he is still trusted by the warden of the prison. The text indicates time passing by simply saying "after these things," but we may ask, How long after Joseph was falsely accused by Potiphar's wife were the chief cupbearer and the chief baker thrown in prison? I suggest that about a year has transpired. (Remember in chapter 3 that I promised to explain the timing of these things. And I will. Later.)

Two officers of the court "offended" Pharaoh (literally "sinned against" in the Hebrew) and as a result incur his wrath. These two officials filled critical roles in the royal court:

Chief cupbearer: taster, confidant (see Nehemiah 1:11;
    Nehemiah was cupbearer to the Persian king Artaxerxes)
Chief baker: royal food preparer

In the ancient world, there were basically two ways to become the king. First was to be born the son of the king and then assume the throne after your father's death. The second way was to assassinate the king and then take over the throne. One of the primary methods of assassinating the king was by poisoning. With palace intrigue and assassination plots not uncommon in the ancient world, the roles of cupbearer and baker represented positions of absolute trust. The person who hands you your cup and the person who prepares your food are very important people in your life—and must be absolutely above suspicion.

For some reason that the text does not divulge, Pharaoh became angry with these two once-trusted officials and has them both imprisoned. The word "prison" refers to a dungeon or roundhouse with no windows. It was a dark, smelly, stifling place—a hard place, especially for those accustomed to the luxury of life in the palace.

What happens next is a clear picture of the sovereign God at work. They are put in the prison where Joseph is, and Joseph is given care over them. Notice by whom—"the captain of the bodyguard" (v. 4). That is Potiphar (see 39:1)! Joseph then, showing the significance of their positions, serves them. What a coincidence, you might say—they ended up with Joseph.

To me, there is no such thing as coincidence. Since God is in control, nothing is an accident. Everything happens for a purpose.

Do you view life as if God is involved? Do you seek to see the invisible hand of God in all of life's circumstances? He is fully engaged in our lives!

When I was in Bible college, it was a small school with a limited talent pool, which meant there were opportunities for those who were willing but perhaps without a huge amount of talent—like me. As such, I found myself on a traveling ministry team doing dramatic speeches and, at the same time, on the school's soccer team as the starting goalkeeper. In the fall of 1975, I had a rally scheduled on the same day as a soccer match. So I went to the director of the ministry team and said I would have to miss the rally to play in the soccer game. He was completely unflustered by this and wished me well. But then two days later, in a different soccer match, I suffered a separated shoulder and would be forced to miss the match on the conflict date.

So I went back to the ministry leader and said I could go after all. He was again underwhelming in his response. When the time came to board the bus for the rally—which was in Niagara Falls, New York—I noticed a truly beautiful girl on the bus. I found a seat next to a friend and began to pepper him with questions about her, finding out her name and a little bit of her story.

That girl was Marlene Dickenson, who is now Marlene Crowder. We have been married over forty-five years, have five children and nine grandchildren, and are just starting to dip our toes into the great-grandparent space.

What's my point? The point is that I found out later that she wasn't even supposed to be on that trip. She was tapped at the last minute as a replacement in the choir. Marlene and I met on a trip that neither of us was supposed to be on! What some might view as a coincidence we saw as the providential, sovereign hand of our loving God to bring us together. As Søren Kierkegaard said, "Life can only be understood backwards; but it must be lived forwards." Looking backward, God's faithful hand can be clearly seen in our experience.

So, no, I do not believe in coincidence because I believe in God.

In a similar way, Joseph and these two court officers do not arrive in the same place by accident or by coincidence. It is another step in God's unfolding of his perfect plans—both for Joseph and for the world.

There are no accidents; there are only divine appointments. If you refuse to see the matchless hand of God in the circumstances of life, you will miss the great blessing of knowing that He is at work—not just sometimes, not just when things work out the way we like, but always.

Joseph and these men converge in prison right on schedule in the perfect plan of God, and God will accomplish His purposes through this divine appointment!

## A Desire to Serve (Genesis 40:5–19)

As followers of Christ, we are called to serve—as our Lord Himself set the example for us, both in word and deed:

> Jesus called them to Himself and said, "You know that the rulers of the Gentiles domineer over them, and those in high position exercise authority over them. It is not this way among you, but whoever wants to become prominent among you shall be your servant, and whoever desires to be first among you shall be your slave; just as the Son of Man did not come to be served, but to serve, and to give His life a ransom for many." (Matthew 20:25–28; see Mark 9:35; 10:43)

> If anyone serves Me, he must follow Me; and where I am, there My servant will be also; if anyone serves Me, the Father will honor him. (John 12:26)

> But it is not this way for you; rather the one who is the greatest among you must become like the youngest, and the leader like the servant. (Luke 22:26)

That is all well and good, but serving doesn't come naturally to us. In general, we prefer being served. There is something embedded deeply within us that wants to be on top. Joseph had been on top in Potiphar's household—or at least as on top as a slave could be. Now he is back in the lowly place: a prisoner, but one trusted by the warden.

### *Dreams in the Night* (v. 5)

> Then the cupbearer and the baker for the king of Egypt, who were confined in the prison, both had a dream the same night, each man with his own dream and each dream with its own interpretation.

The ancient Egyptians, like many ancient cultures, placed great stock in dreams and their significance, viewing them as messages from the gods. In prison, however, these two court officers were cut off from the wise men and the dream interpreters, so they were distressed. They wanted to know the meaning of their dreams, but this was beyond them. They were without resources—or so they thought.

### *Ready to Help* (vv. 6–7)

> When Joseph came to them in the morning and saw them, behold, they were dejected. So he asked Pharaoh's officials who were with him in confinement in his master's house, "Why are your faces so sad today?"

Don't miss this. It is one of my favorite moments in the Joseph story. Joseph has learned to be sensitive to others—a drastic change from when he was a teen in Canaan and did not see how his favored status and spectacular dreams affected his brothers. In spite of his own hardship and difficulty (or perhaps because of it), he recognizes the hurt and distress of the cupbearer and baker. He not only sees their sadness and is concerned, but Joseph cares enough to get involved. There is a tremendous insight here. Joseph has continued to learn, and learn well, for his response to unjust imprisonment is twofold:

Vertical response: He has not allowed his circumstances to disrupt his relationship with the Lord (see 39:21, 23).

Horizontal response: He has not allowed his own hurt to keep him from helping others who hurt.

Let's face it, Joseph could have ignored them. I can only imagine what my response might have been in that situation. "Who cares? I have enough pain of my own. I have enough problems of my own. When someone starts caring about my hurt, maybe I will care about them."

But Joseph didn't do that. He set aside his personal adversity to help others who were hurting. That is not only servant ministry—it is good therapy! Remember Elijah, on the run from Jezebel, when he groveled in self-pity and asked God to take his life (1 Kings 19:4). It was the only recorded prayer of Elijah that God didn't answer. In fact, God never answered it, for Elijah departed this world without the experience of death (2 Kings 2). What God did instead was give Elijah a project to invest himself into—Elisha. Elijah's job was to train and prepare his replacement for when it was his time to depart the world. The lesson is clear—there is great value in taking our eyes off of our own pain to give ourselves to others.

> **There is great value in taking our eyes off of our own pain to give ourselves to others.**

Elijah's story reminds me of Jim and Phyllis, a couple who could not have children, but instead of grieving their infertility, they adopted a daughter (who went on to become my wife) and a son. They invested in those children whose lives would have been dramatically different, and quite possibly much worse, had they not looked beyond their disappointment and seen the needs of two little ones.

Is that how you respond to adversity? Or are you so consumed with your own pain and self-pity that you are unable (or unwilling) to see the pain of others? Sensitivity to the hurts of others can be killed by an obsession with personal misfortune. Not so with Joseph. He cares and is concerned. He notices and gets involved.

### *Discussion of the Dreams* (vv. 8–19)

> And they said to him, "We have had a dream, and there is no one to interpret it." Then Joseph said to them, "Do interpretations not belong to God? Tell it to me, please."
>
> So the chief cupbearer told his dream to Joseph, saying to him, "In my dream, behold, there was a vine in front of me; and on the vine were three branches. And as it was budding, its blossoms came out, and its clusters produced ripe grapes. Now Pharaoh's cup was in my hand; so I took the grapes and squeezed them into Pharaoh's cup, and I put the cup into Pharaoh's hand." Then Joseph said to him, "This is the interpretation of it: the three branches are three days; within three more days Pharaoh will lift up your head and restore you to your office; and you will put Pharaoh's cup into his hand as in your former practice when you were his cupbearer. Only keep me in mind when it goes well with you, and please do me a kindness by mentioning me to Pharaoh, and get me out of this prison. For I was in fact kidnapped from the land

of the Hebrews, and even here I have done nothing
that they should have put me into the dungeon."

When the chief baker saw that he had interpreted
favorably, he said to Joseph, "I also saw in my
dream, and behold, there were three baskets of white
bread on my head; and in the top basket there were
some of all kinds of baked food for Pharaoh, and
the birds were eating them out of the basket on my
head." Then Joseph answered and said, "This is
its interpretation: the three baskets are three days;
within three more days Pharaoh will lift up your
head from you and will hang you on a wooden
post, and the birds will eat your flesh off you."

"Do interpretations not belong to God?" Joseph asked (v. 8).
We see yet another contrast to chapter 37 when Joseph lorded his
dreams over his brothers. Not now. Now Joseph trusts in God, not
himself. He makes it abundantly clear that he is not clairvoyant
or some kind of seer. He openly declares his dependence upon his
God and asks them to share their dreams.

The royal cupbearer is up first. He describes seeing in his dream
a three-branched vine with buds, blossoms, and grapes. In the
dream, he made juice and put it into Pharaoh's cup and then gave
it to Pharaoh.

Joseph's interpretation is immediate. The three branches equal
three days. In three days' time, the cupbearer will be restored to
his former position.

Then Joseph does something very interesting. He makes a request,
asking the cupbearer for mercy and remembrance when he is rein-
stated. Joseph explains his innocence. The key here is that there are
times when it is proper to say a word in your own defense. In Acts
22, for instance, Paul was arrested and was about to be flogged

by a Roman commander. Before that could happen, however, Paul made it clear that he was a freeborn Roman citizen. Immediately, the whip was put away. Though God is ultimately the vindicator, there is a time to say a word about your innocence (if you are innocent). Just be careful to leave the outcomes in God's hands.

Joseph made his request and then moved to the baker and his dream.

In his dream, the baker sees three baskets on top of his head, with the top basket filled with "all kinds of baked food for Pharaoh" (v. 17). In my imagination I see rich, delicious pastries, carefully prepared to present to the king. However, birds, which sometimes in the Scriptures are symbolic of evil (Matthew 13:4, 19), are eating the pastries out of the top basket.

Once again, Joseph interprets the dream without hesitation. The three baskets equal three days. In three days, the baker will lose his head, be hanged (that is, impaled) on a stake, and scavenged by birds.

It is interesting that Joseph is confident enough of his interpretation that he makes no request of the baker, as he had from the cupbearer.

## Developing Patience (Genesis 40:20–23)

> So it came about on the third day, which was Pharaoh's birthday, that he held a feast for all his servants; and he lifted up the head of the chief cupbearer and the head of the chief baker among his servants. He restored the chief cupbearer to his office, and he put the cup into Pharaoh's hand; but he hanged the chief baker, just as Joseph had interpreted to them. Yet the chief cupbearer did not remember Joseph, but forgot him.

In verse 20, we find the significance of the third day. It was Pharaoh's birthday! He throws a feast for his servants and recalls from prison the cupbearer and baker to share in the celebration. At his birthday party, Pharaoh restores the cupbearer to his former position of trust and executes the baker, just as Joseph said.

In another case of the saying "No good deed goes unpunished," verse 23 tells us that "the chief cupbearer did not remember Joseph." Joseph's sensitivity was rewarded with insensitivity, as his purity had been rewarded by treachery in his experience with Mrs. Potiphar. How long would he be forgotten? "Two full years" (41:1)!

Joseph is abandoned, this time not by an enemy (Potiphar's wife) but by a friend. By someone he had helped when that man was in distress. This time he is abandoned for a long time, not a short time.

The cupbearer forgot him, and it is a warning to us as well. Far too often in the midst of our joy and freedom and prosperity, we forget others too. Joseph is forgotten and in danger of falling into disillusionment—a terribly damaging attitude. As one Bible teacher said, "Disillusionment is caused by placing your trust and hope in men, but it is cured by placing all of your trust and hope in God!"

Joseph was sensitive to others who weren't sensitive to him and his needs. He could have become bitter and unforgiving, but he was trusting instead. Why? Because, though the cupbearer had forgotten him, God hadn't! See how Joseph's life had played out to this point:

At seventeen, he is sold into slavery by his brothers.

At twenty-seven, he is falsely accused and imprisoned.

At twenty-eight, he is forgotten by a man he helped.

At thirty, he will be suddenly discovered.

Joseph is learning that patience comes from knowing God and trusting Him. As a result, at age thirty, Joseph will become an overnight success that took God thirteen years to build. James 1 says that this patience is a key attitude for spiritual growth. Without patience, there will be no maturity—and without delays, trials, and disappointments, there will be no patience (vv. 2–4). Joseph's faith has produced a faithfulness in trials that produces a patience that will make him mature. The great Bible commentator F. B. Meyer wrote:

> As a boy, Joseph's character tended to softness. He was a little spoilt by his father. He was too proud . . . of his dreams and foreshadowed greatness. None of these were great faults; but he lacked strength, grip, power to rule. But what a difference his imprisonment made in him! From that moment he carries himself with a wisdom, modesty, courage, and manly resolution, that never fail him. . . . He has learned to hold his peace and wait. Surely the iron had entered his soul![2]

Now he is ready. And his preparation was fueled by patient trust in the Lord—a lesson we would also do well to learn. As Louisa M. Stead wrote:

> 'Tis so sweet to trust in Jesus,
> And to take Him at His Word;
> Just to rest upon His promise
> And to know, "Thus saith the Lord."
>
> Jesus, Jesus, how I trust Him!
> How I've proved Him o'er and o'er!
> Jesus, Jesus, precious Jesus!
> O for grace to trust Him more!

I'm so glad I learned to trust Him,
Precious Jesus, Savior, Friend;
And I know that He is with me,
Will be with me to the end.

And that is the key. As He was with Joseph, our Lord will be with us all the way to the end. We can patiently trust Him for the outcomes and the timing of those outcomes.

## Questions for Personal Reflection or Group Discussion

1. How can personal pain prepare us for serving others? How can personal pain prevent us from serving others?
2. When has personal pain impacted you negatively? Positively?
3. How can our own struggles equip us to encourage others (see 2 Corinthians 1:3–7)?
4. As an introvert, I tend to withdraw when I am hurting. How do you respond to such times?
5. When has someone else reached out to help you in your seasons of struggle?

# 6

# SUCCESS AT LAST

### GENESIS 41

Jimmy Morris may not be a household name for most baseball fans, but his story is one for the ages. He had long dreamed of pitching in the major leagues, but that dream had been back-burnered by the demands of life. Married with three children, Jimmy was a high school teacher and baseball coach of the Big Lake Owls high school team. When he encouraged his floundering high school players to try harder, they challenged him: if they made it out of the district tournament and to the state playoffs, he had to try out for the majors.

Shockingly, they succeeded, and even more shockingly, when Jimmy tried out for the Tampa Bay Devil Rays, he was signed to a contract. It was still a long path to the Show (the big leagues), but he battled through the minors and finally got called up to pitch for the major league club. At age thirty-five, Jimmy Morris became an overnight success—and it only took a dozen or so years to get there. Though he did not pitch for long in the majors, his story is an inspiration to many aspiring ballplayers and is beautifully told in the film *The Rookie*, one of my favorite baseball movies.

Success may seem to come easily to some, but for most it is a long process, as it was for Jimmy Morris—and as it was for our friend Joseph. Yet, through slavery, false imprisonment, and years of being forgotten, all along the Lord was with him and brought him from the darkest of places to a place of honor and regard. As Fanny Crosby wrote:

> All the way my Savior leads me—
> What have I to ask beside?
> Can I doubt His faithful mercies,
> Who through life has been my guide?
> Heavenly peace, divinest comfort,
> Here by faith in Him to dwell!
> For I know, whate'er befall me,
> Jesus doeth all things well.

Our God does all things well, which is why, after thirteen years of reversals, failure, and treachery, the light of day enters Joseph's jail cell.

After aiding the royal cupbearer, Joseph was forgotten again, this time for two full years (Genesis 41:1). Two more years of suffering, pain, and solitude, yes—but more importantly, two more years of preparation and construction in the life of this future leader, preparation that enables Joseph to become a success at last. Now the time has come for which God has been preparing this servant.

It can't be ignored that everything that has happened to this point has led to this: Joseph rising to a position of authority and power for the purpose of saving the world, including his own family.

### Pharaoh's Dreams (Genesis 41:1–8)

> Now it happened at the end of two full years that
> Pharaoh had a dream, and behold, he was standing

by the Nile. And behold, from the Nile seven cows came up, fine-looking and fat; and they grazed in the marsh grass. Then behold, seven other cows came up after them from the Nile, ugly and thin, and they stood by the other cows on the bank of the Nile. Then the ugly and thin cows ate the seven fine-looking and fat cows. Then Pharaoh awoke. But he fell asleep and dreamed a second time; and behold, seven ears of grain came up on a single stalk, plump and good. Then behold, seven ears, thin and scorched by the east wind, sprouted up after them. The thin ears swallowed the seven plump and full ears. Then Pharaoh awoke, and behold, it was a dream. Now in the morning his spirit was troubled, so he sent messengers and called for all the soothsayer priests of Egypt, and all its wise men. And Pharaoh told them his dreams, but there was no one who could interpret them for Pharaoh.

Note again the time marker "at the end of two full years" (v. 1). Two full years during which Joseph continued to be imprisoned unjustly. At the end of that time, however, Pharaoh had a pair of dreams that disturbed him greatly.

In the first dream, Pharaoh stood by the Nile River—which was viewed as a god by the ancient Egyptians—and saw seven fat cows leave the water. This was not at all unusual. People often saw cows in the water to escape the heat and the flies. So far, so good.

As the seven fat and healthy cows emerged from the water, however, seven ugly and gaunt cows eat them. This is frightening because this is unnatural behavior. Cows don't eat beef! Cows are beef; they don't eat beef.

After this disturbing dream, Pharaoh awakened—startled by

what he saw in the dream. But then Pharaoh went back to sleep and dreamed again.

In this dream, he saw seven good ears of grain—healthy and health-giving. Once again, however, the tables turn as seven blighted, diseased, and wind-damaged ears of grain come and consume the good ears. This also is frightening because inanimate things have taken on the characteristics of animate things. Like a macabre Disney cartoon where things that aren't supposed to take on life do, the dream again startles Pharaoh and he awakes.

As we saw in the previous chapter, ancient Egyptians placed great value on dreams, believing them to contain messages from the gods. As such, Pharaoh was troubled, as the cupbearer and baker had been two years before. He sensed that these dreams were more than just dreams. So he sent for the wise men and magicians to interpret the dreams—but none could interpret the dreams for him.

There is an important lesson here about the great danger in seeking spiritual answers in the wrong places. As in Daniel 2, we see a genuine hunger in the human heart for spiritual answers, for spiritual truth—yet there is a great tragedy in filling the void from the wrong sources.

There are more false teachers and leaders, more cults and isms than ever before, yet as Solomon said of life in general, it is all vanity (Ecclesiastes 1:2). Human wisdom is void of the power to address the needs and questions of the human heart. There is only emptiness in human answers. Answers must be sought based on what God has revealed, and until we are willing to accept God's truth and its authority over our lives, we will not have the answers to the things that trouble our hearts and stir our souls.

Pharaoh was no doubt greatly disappointed by the failure of his spiritual advisers, but their failure opened the door for God's man—Joseph.

## The Cupbearer's Decision (Genesis 41:9–13)

> Then the chief cupbearer spoke to Pharaoh, saying,
> "I would make mention today of my own offenses.
> Pharaoh was furious with his servants, and he put
> me in confinement in the house of the captain of
> the bodyguard, both me and the chief baker. Then
> we had a dream one night, he and I; each of us
> dreamed according to the interpretation of his own
> dream. Now a Hebrew youth was there with us,
> a servant of the captain of the bodyguard, and we
> told him the dreams, and he interpreted our dreams
> for us. For each man he interpreted according to
> his own dream. And just as he interpreted for us,
> so it happened; Pharaoh restored me in my office,
> but he hanged the chief baker."

As the royal cupbearer, this man would have been at Pharaoh's side and heard everything as the king recounted his dreams to the wise men and priests. The cupbearer remembers his failings regarding Joseph and readily confesses them. He explains the situation to Pharaoh and tells him of the interpreter who answered his questions two years before in prison. Now Joseph will come into contact with the third in a trilogy of dream pairs:

First, the pair of dreams Joseph had regarding dominion over
    his brothers
Second, the dreams paired by the baker and cupbearer
Third, Pharaoh's pair of dreams

It is really interesting to see how these dreams fit together for Joseph. The second pair of dreams (the cupbearer's and baker's) enable him to come into contact with the third pair of dreams

(Pharaoh's), which make possible the fulfillment of the first pair of dreams (Joseph's own). They are all linked together by the sovereign hand of God.

The promises God gave Joseph thirteen years before have now come full circle. To our eyes, this fulfillment may seem to be about thirteen years too late, but in the wise plan of God, it is right on time—when God always knew it would be. It all sets the stage for the first of two times (the second being Moses) when God used a Hebrew slave to confound the Egyptians.

## Joseph's Deliverance (Genesis 41:14–16)

> Then Pharaoh sent word and called for Joseph, and they hurriedly brought him out of the dungeon; and when he had shaved himself and changed his clothes, he came to Pharaoh. Pharaoh said to Joseph, "I have had a dream, but no one can interpret it; and I have heard it said about you, that when you hear a dream you can interpret it." Joseph then answered Pharaoh, saying, "It has nothing to do with me; God will give Pharaoh an answer for his own good."

Pharaoh has no other options, so he calls Joseph. And with Joseph's liberation, we see his godly character undiminished by unfair treatment and years in prison.

First, we see Joseph's *dignity*. He shaves in preparation for meeting the most powerful man in the land. This matters because Egyptians were clean-shaven while Hebrews were normally bearded. Joseph then changes clothes before coming before Pharaoh. You can only imagine how his clothes smelled after about three years in prison. Yet, in spite of the mistreatment he received, Joseph has a sense of dignity, propriety, and decorum that his years in prison could not extinguish. He comes before Pharaoh to hear the great ruler's dilemma—a dilemma that will be Joseph's deliverance—but he still displays godly character, not self-centered arrogance.

Second, we see Joseph's *humility*. Pharaoh begins by establishing the ground rules: "I have had a dream, but no one can interpret it; and I have heard it said about you, that when you hear a dream you can interpret it" (v. 15). The king must have been stunned with surprise to hear Joseph's answer: "It has nothing to do with me" (v. 16). Joseph doesn't use his big moment to try to impress Pharaoh or make grandiose claims about himself (though he might have back in Genesis 37). After all that has happened, Joseph has learned to place his confidence not in himself but in the Lord—and that is a profound lesson. Hence, the rest of his reply to Pharaoh's concerns is, "God will give Pharaoh an answer for his own good" (v. 16).

Joseph witnesses to his faith, gives God the glory, and displays a boldness uncharacteristic of a typical, run-of-the-mill prisoner. Living in the presence of God has made a profound difference in Joseph's life, and he uses the moment to point to his God rather than to himself. In this is wisdom. As Scottish pastor and theologian James Denney said, "No man can give at once the impressions that he himself is clever and that Jesus Christ is mighty to save."[1] Joseph's focus is on his Lord.

God's patient—and painful—investment and work in the life of Joseph has paid off. These first words spoken by Joseph after exiting prison show that his lessons have been well learned.

### Pharaoh's Dreams (Genesis 41:17–36)

> So Pharaoh said to Joseph, "In my dream, there I was, standing on the bank of the Nile; and behold, seven cows, fat and fine-looking came up out of

the Nile, and they grazed in the marsh grass. Then behold, seven other cows came up after them, poor and very ugly and thin, such as I had never seen for ugliness in all the land of Egypt; and the thin and ugly cows ate the first seven fat cows. Yet when they had devoured them, it could not be detected that they had devoured them, for they were just as ugly as before. Then I awoke. I saw also in my dream, and behold, seven ears of grain, full and good, came up on a single stalk; and behold, seven ears of grain, withered, thin, and scorched by the east wind sprouted up after them; and the thin ears swallowed the seven good ears. Then I told it to the soothsayer priests, but there was no one who could explain it to me." (vv. 17–24)

Pharaoh tells the dream of the cows and the dream of the grain, and interestingly he tells them with more detail than he did (probably several hours earlier) to the wise men. All of us dream, but in my experience, what is vivid when I first awake fades into oblivion as time passes. Not here. Pharaoh gives more detail now than he did earlier, perhaps indicating the degree to which these dreams have shaken him.

Pharaoh then adds that no one could explain the meaning of these things. This is critical—human failures open a door of opportunity for the glory of God to be clearly displayed. What is beyond human reason is not beyond God.

### Joseph Explains the Dreams to Pharaoh (vv. 25–32)

And Joseph said to Pharaoh, "Pharaoh's dreams are one and the same; God has told to Pharaoh what He is about to do. The seven good cows are seven years; and the seven good ears are seven years; the dreams are one and the same. The seven thin and ugly cows that came up after them are seven years, and the seven thin ears scorched by the east wind will be seven years of famine. It is as I have spoken to Pharaoh: God has shown Pharaoh what He is about to do. Behold, seven years of great abundance are coming in all the land of Egypt; and after them seven years of famine will come, and all the abundance will be forgotten in the land of Egypt, and the famine will ravage the land. So the abundance will be unknown in the land because of that subsequent famine; for it will be very severe. Now as for the repeating of the dream to Pharaoh twice, it means that the matter is confirmed by God, and God will quickly bring it about.

> The ultimate lesson taught to Joseph by slavery, treachery, imprisonment, and disappointment is the same lesson learned by Job through pain and hardship: God is in control.

The two dreams are actually one dream:

Seven good cows and ears of grain = seven good years of plentiful harvest
Seven bad cows and ears of grain = seven bad years of famine

"God has told to Pharaoh what He is about to do," Joseph concludes (v. 25). The double dream is confirmed by the Lord—it will happen. Why? Because God is God, and He is orchestrating the circumstances and events of life to His desired ends. The ultimate lesson taught to Joseph by slavery, treachery, imprisonment, and disappointment is the same lesson learned by Job through pain and hardship: God is in control. He will do what He says and accomplish what He has set forth. He is God, and He is in charge. Joseph challenges Pharaoh to see the sovereignty of God and to begin planning on the basis of what God is doing.

With this, Joseph gives us a critical principle if we are to serve God. Like Joseph, we must learn to see the sovereignty of God in all our lives.

### Joseph's Counsel to Pharaoh (vv. 33–36)

> So now let Pharaoh look for a man discerning and wise, and appoint him over the land of Egypt. Let Pharaoh take action to appoint overseers in charge of the land, and let him take a fifth of the produce of the land of Egypt as a tax in the seven years of abundance. Then have them collect all the food of these good years that are coming, and store up the grain for food in the cities under Pharaoh's authority, and have them guard it. Let the food be used as a reserve for the land for the seven years of famine which will occur in the land of Egypt, so that the land will not perish during the famine.

Joseph's speech is bold and not a little risky. A slave and prisoner giving unsolicited advice to the king could be seen as presumption—even an insult. But Joseph offers counsel anyway: Find a man, wise and discreet, and put him in charge. Take one fifth of the food for the seven good years and store it away for the seven lean years. This is great counsel.

British Prime Minister William Gladstone (1809–1898), when asked what the mark of a great statesman is, said, "A man who knows the way God is going for the next fifty years."[2] No one else in Egypt knew what God was up to, but Joseph did, and his counsel—unsolicited though it was—was gladly received by Pharaoh.

## Pharaoh's Decision (Genesis 41:37–45)

Pharaoh sees the truth and wisdom of Joseph's interpretation and counsel and responds by implementing Joseph's plan—in a surprising way. He appoints Joseph himself to oversee the preparation for the coming famine that is still seven years away.

### *The Qualifications of Joseph* (vv. 37–39)

> Now the proposal seemed good to Pharaoh and to all his servants.
>
> Then Pharaoh said to his servants, "Can we find a man like this, in whom there is a divine spirit?" So Pharaoh said to Joseph, "Since God has informed you of all this, there is no one as discerning and wise as you are."

Hear Pharaoh describe the qualities of a leader: indwelled with divine Spirit, listens to God, has discernment. As in Acts 6 and 1 Timothy 3, the key character qualities of leadership, which took years of suffering to develop in Joseph, are internal, not external. They deal with knowing God, not being great.

The key behind it all? God's sovereign timing was perfect once again. Two years previously, when Joseph interpreted the court officials' dreams, his ability to interpret dreams would have been an oddity and a curiosity. But now, in response to the nation's

> **The key character qualities of leadership, which took years of suffering to develop in Joseph, are internal, not external.**

need and in the light of human failure, it is the instrument of God to spare the nation and to keep His promises to Joseph.

This former slave is now raised to the position God promised him thirteen years before when he was a youth in Canaan. You cannot argue with the timing of God once you recognize its absolute perfection.

### *The Exaltation of Joseph* (vv. 40–45)

> "You shall be in charge of my house, and all my people shall be obedient to you; only regarding the throne will I be greater than you." Pharaoh said to Joseph, "See, I have placed you over all the land of Egypt." Then Pharaoh took off his signet ring from his hand and put it on Joseph's hand, and clothed him in garments of fine linen, and put the gold necklace around his neck. And he had him ride in his second chariot; and they proclaimed ahead him, "Bow the knee!" And he placed him over all the land of Egypt. Moreover, Pharaoh said to Joseph, "Though I am Pharaoh, yet without your permission no one shall raise his hand or foot in all the land of Egypt." Then Pharaoh named Joseph Zaphenath-paneah; and he gave him Asenath, the daughter of Potiphera priest of On, to be his wife. And Joseph went out over the land of Egypt.

Several things happen as a result of Pharaoh's decision.

First, Joseph is placed over Pharaoh's house, as he was over Potiphar's house before. His position is similar to that of a prime minister, second only to Pharaoh in authority over the land. And Joseph was to be honored wherever he went in the land as Pharaoh's second-in-command.

Second, Joseph is given a signet ring of authority (used to seal royal documents with wax), clothes, and jewelry. All of this greatly contrasts with the harshness, rags, and chains of slavery and prison that he endured for the last thirteen years.

Third, Joseph is given a new name and a wife. The name? Zaphenath-paneah—"one to whom God reveals secrets." The wife? Asenath, daughter of Potiphera, priest of On.

From the privations of slavery and prison to abundance as the head of Pharaoh's court. From loneliness and isolation to a new family and home. Joseph's head must have been spinning with this massive turnaround in his fortunes. He was experiencing in real time what Paul described in Ephesians 3:20:

> Now to Him who is able to do far more abundantly beyond all that we ask or think, according to the power that works within us . . .

Joseph experienced this abundance firsthand as his faithful God kept His promises to him.

## Joseph's Duty (Genesis 41:46–49)

> Now Joseph was thirty years old when he stood in the presence of Pharaoh, king of Egypt. And Joseph went out from the presence of Pharaoh and went through all the land of Egypt. During the seven years of plenty the land produced abundantly. So he collected all the food of these seven years which occurred in the land of Egypt and put the food in the cities; he put in every city the food from its own surrounding fields. Joseph stored up grain in great abundance like the sand of the sea, until he stopped measuring it, for it was beyond measure.

Joseph was thirty years old. Sit with that for a minute. Thirteen years had passed since he was sold into slavery. Now think of where you were and what you were doing thirteen years ago. As I reflect on the last thirteen years, in that period of time I have lost my mom, my mother-in-law, a brother, two sisters, and a sister-in-law. I'm sure you have experienced your own levels of change. Thirteen years is a long time!

For Joseph, this was not just time passed or time spent—it was time invested. He learned and matured and grew and developed. Even the time he spent running Potiphar's household contributed to the logistical and organizational skills Joseph later needed for his massive world-saving task. But remember what it took to get him here:

> And [God] called for a famine upon the land;
> He broke the whole staff of bread.
> He sent a man before them,
> Joseph, who was sold as a slave.
> They forced his feet into shackles,
> He was put in irons;
> Until the time that his word came to pass,
> The word of the LORD refined him.
> The king sent and released him,
> The ruler of peoples, and set him free.
> He made him lord of his house,
> And ruler over all his possessions,
> To imprison his high officials at will,
> That he might teach his elders wisdom.
>                              (Psalm 105:16–22)

Now all of that time pays off as Joseph, having learned the lessons of those thirteen years, takes charge of gathering and storing the grain of the seven abundant years in anticipation of the seven years of famine.

## The Sons of Joseph (Genesis 41:50–52)

> Now before the year of famine came, two sons were
> born to Joseph, whom Asenath, the daughter of
> Potiphera, priest of On, bore to him. Joseph named
> the firstborn Manasseh; "For," he said, "God has
> made me forget all my trouble and all of my father's
> household." And he named the second Ephraim;
> "For," he said, "God has made me fruitful in the
> land of my affliction."

Joseph and his wife, Asenath, have two sons, and—proving
that he has not forgotten his heritage or his God—he gives them
Hebrew names:

Manasseh: "forgetting"; the pain of the past is forgotten.
Ephraim: "fruitful"; fruitfulness has come from affliction.

One of my favorite Bible teachers, Dr. J. Vernon McGee, called
them "Amnesia" and "Ambrosia."[3] The pain and loneliness are
buried, and joy is restored. The years of faithfulness and learning
have been worth it.

## The Famine Begins (Genesis 41:53–57)

> When the seven years of plenty which had taken
> place in the land of Egypt came to an end, and the
> seven years of famine began to come, just as Joseph
> had said, then there was famine in all the lands; but
> in all the land of Egypt there was bread. So when
> all the land of Egypt suffered famine, the people
> cried out to Pharaoh for bread; and Pharaoh said
> to all the Egyptians, "Go to Joseph; whatever he

says to you, you shall do." When the famine was spread over the entire face of the earth, then Joseph opened all the storehouses and sold grain to the Egyptians; and the famine was severe in the land of Egypt. Then the people of all the earth came to Egypt to buy grain from Joseph, because the famine was severe in all the earth.

As Joseph predicted, and right on time, the famine begins. Due to the plentiful good years, Joseph can now sell the grain for a profit to the world. At age thirty-eight when the famine hits, Joseph is used by God to feed the world. Years of failure are answered with the joy of being God's instrument. Which brings forward another important lesson:

Hang in there—it is always too soon to quit!

In the 1924 Olympics, Eric Liddell, the flying Scotsman who went on to be a missionary in China, set world and Olympic records in the four-hundred-meter dash—a race for which he had never trained. When questioned about his victory, Liddell reportedly said, "I ran the first 200 yards as hard as I could. Then, by God's strength, I ran the next 200 yards harder!"

That same level of God-reliant determination brought Joseph to where he was. Very often, success is found in dealing rightly with crisis. Joseph had learned well and now was a fitting leader—ready for the pressure, the task, and the assault on his heart—because God had prepared him well. No wonder, for he was forged in the fires. Bible teacher A. W. Tozer said, "It is doubtful whether God can bless a man greatly until He has hurt him deeply."[4] Samuel Rutherford agreed: "O, what owe I to the file, to the hammer, to the furnace of my Lord Jesus! Who hath now let me see how good the wheat of Christ is, that goeth through His mill and His oven, to be made bread for His own table." [5]

Joseph experienced it all and now is ready to be used of God. Are you? Beyond that, are you ready and willing to accept what it may take to get you ready? There is no other way to be prepared for true spiritual success in a fallen world. Trials are part of life, but how we respond to them makes all the difference.

As Catharina von Schlegel wrote in 1697:

> Be still, my soul: the Lord is on thy side;
> Bear patiently the cross of grief or pain.
> Leave to thy God to order and provide;
> In every change He faithful will remain.
> Be still, my soul: thy best, thy heavenly Friend
> Through thorny ways leads to a joyful end.
>
> Be still, my soul: thy God doth undertake
> To guide the future as He has the past.
> Thy hope, thy confidence let nothing shake;
> All now mysterious shall be bright at last.
> Be still, my soul: the waves and winds still know
> His voice who ruled them while He dwelt below.

Great words—words that describe Joseph's trust in his God through the darkest of times, and now into a new set of challenges . . .

> Then the people of all the earth came to Egypt to buy grain from Joseph, because the famine was severe in all the earth. (v. 57)

"All the earth" includes Canaan, where his family is. Guess who's coming to dinner?

## Questions for Personal Reflection or Group Discussion

1. Consider where you were thirteen years ago. What has changed in your life during those years? Think of how long that period of time must have been for Joseph.

2. Which stands out to you more about Joseph's appearance before Pharaoh, his dignity or his humility? How could those have been dulled by his years in captivity?

3. On a human level, Joseph took a risk admitting he did not personally have the ability to interpret Pharaoh's dreams. How does this risk reveal Joseph's confidence and trust in his God?

4. Recognizing the importance of names in ancient times, how do the names given to Joseph's sons reflect his heart for God?

5. We often hear today that one person can't make a difference in our world. How does Joseph's story offer hope that individuals do matter—especially in God's plans?

# 7

# IN THE COURSE OF WORLD EVENTS

## GENESIS 42

As sovereign, God has the ability and prerogative to orchestrate world events to accomplish His purposes. In the case of the worldwide famine recorded in Genesis, God's global purposes included His purposes for Joseph and his estranged family.

It has been about twenty-two years since Joseph was sold into slavery. And Joseph has absolute confidence that God has been at work in Egypt. His amazing rise from slave to ruler gives indisputable evidence of divine sovereignty in his life. The question, however, is whether or not God has likewise been at work in Canaan—the old homeland.

Joseph has the world by the tail with a downhill swing, but there are some loose ends that must be resolved. Some of them have to do with reconciliation, some with forgiveness, and some with the human tendency toward bitterness when we are mistreated by people we trusted.

For Joseph's brothers, they have had to live with their guilt for twenty-two years. For twenty-two years they have deceived their

97

father. For twenty-two years they have hidden their sin. But what goes around does come around. As we have already seen, what one (or a group of ones) sows, one will most definitely reap (Galatians 6:7). Over the twenty-two years there must have been times when the brothers wanted to tell—to confess to their father what they had done. The years of silent guilt no doubt took a toll on them individually and on the family as a whole. Now it is time to lance this festering boil and get the poison out. Though it will be painful in the short term, it is utterly necessary if they are to heal.

For Joseph, this will also test his character. How much has he learned and grown? How much does he trust the God who has brought him to this position of authority? How much will he be able to forgive? Have the twenty-plus years of hardship taught him not to be hardened?

We will find out. Joseph has experienced thirteen years of slavery and imprisonment and seven years of plenty, and now he is in the midst of seven years of famine. In this famine, Joseph's storehouses will feed the world, because the word has spread, "There is food in Egypt!" And word of that possible provision reaches even to Canaan.

## The Undeniable Dream (Genesis 42:1–5)

> Now Jacob saw that there was grain in Egypt, and Jacob said to his sons, "Why are you staring at one another?" Then he said, "Look, I have heard that there is grain in Egypt; go down there and buy some for us from that place, so that we may live and not die." So ten of Joseph's brothers went down to buy grain from Egypt. But Jacob did not send Joseph's brother Benjamin with his brothers, for he said, "I am afraid that harm may happen to him." So

> the sons of Israel came to buy grain among those
> who were coming, because the famine was also in
> the land of Canaan.

This is a classic "meanwhile, back at the ranch . . ." situation. We have been tracking Joseph in Egypt, and now we get our first glimpse of the home front in two decades. Jacob hears that there is food in Egypt. Notice his attitude. Now in old age, he continues to express a life of painful emptiness. In fact, Jacob displays . . .

- *A fatalistic life view:* ". . . so that we may live and not die." Jacob's perspective may seem appropriate under the circumstances they are facing, but not when linked to . . .
- *A faithless life view:* Jacob sees Egypt, *not God*, as his source. As he has done for so much of his life, Jacob is viewing life horizontally rather than factoring in the vertical role of the God of his fathers. Add to that . . .
- *A fruitless life view:* It seems that Jacob hasn't learned a thing over these past twenty-two years. In Genesis 37, Joseph was the favorite. Now Benjamin (Joseph's one full brother) has been elevated to the position of favorite son, and Jacob seems to be just as much in despair as he was when we left him in Genesis 37.

What a bitter old man Jacob must have been. If we compare Genesis 37:34–35 to Genesis 42:1–4, we see that for twenty-two years Jacob has failed to learn how to deal with sorrow, how to trust God, and how to properly parent his sons. He is truly a pitiful case. Jacob was renamed Israel (which means "one who contends with God"), and he wrestled with God as a younger man, but it seems he never learned to trust Him. "Why are you sitting around here being hungry?" Jacob scolds his sons. "Go to Egypt!" So the brothers go to Egypt to find food—but notice that they do so without a word of animosity against Benjamin. Is it possible that the brothers are learning?

God is at work—but Jacob doesn't get it. All he sees is his own pain. Joseph, however, sees God's providence. It is evident in Joseph's rise to power, the worldwide famine, and the inevitable arrival of the brothers looking for food. God is preparing the way for reconciliation, as his servant Joseph feeds the world. God's sovereign working will clean up the ravaged wasteland of this tragic family and restore it. Yet, in all of this, Joseph gets a gut check as well—for he is genuinely caught off guard by his brothers' arrival.

## The Plan for Reconciliation (Genesis 42:6–20)

> Now Joseph was the ruler over the land; he was the one who sold grain to all the people of the land. And Joseph's brothers came and bowed down to him with their faces to the ground. When Joseph saw his brothers, he recognized them, but he disguised himself to them and spoke to them harshly. He said to them, "Where have you come from?" And they said, "From the land of Canaan, to buy food."
>
> But Joseph had recognized his brothers, although they did not recognize him. And Joseph remembered the dreams which he had about them, and he said to them, "You are spies; you have come to look at the undefended parts of our land." And they said to him, "No, my lord, but your servants have come to buy food. We are all sons of one man; we are honest men, your servants are not spies." Yet he said to them, "No, but you have come to look at the undefended parts of our land!" But

they said, "Your servants are twelve brothers in all, the sons of one man in the land of Canaan; and behold, the youngest is with our father today, and one is no longer alive." Yet Joseph said to them, "It is as I said to you, you are spies; by this is you will be tested: by the life of Pharaoh, you shall not leave this place unless your youngest brother comes here! Send one of you and have him get your brother, while you remain confined, so that your words may be tested, whether there is truth in you. But if not, by the life of Pharaoh, you are certainly spies!" So he put them all together in prison for three days.

Now Joseph said to them on the third day, "Do this and live, for I fear God: if you are honest men, let one of your brothers be confined in your prison; but as for the rest of you, go, carry grain for the famine of your households, and bring your youngest brother to me, so that your words may be verified, and you will not die." And they did so.

### *Joseph's Recognition* (vv. 6–8)

Joseph recognizes them, but they don't recognize him. Why? The brothers were older when they sold Joseph away and would have still looked like typical nomadic Hebrews—tanned, weather-beaten, bearded shepherds. Joseph, however, was much younger at their parting, and now twenty-two years later, aging, Egyptian clothing, his skill in the Egyptian language, and, most of all, his role of authority over all of Egypt combine together to make him absolutely unrecognizable. He has gone from seventeen to thirty-nine, from Canaan to Egypt, from slavery to dominion. What a change!

Now Joseph is in charge, and in fulfillment of his dreams

(37:5–9), they are bowing at his feet. He has the perfect opportunity and all the resources in the world with which to take revenge. Will he take the opportunity?

Would you take the opportunity? Would you seek revenge? Look at Joseph's options. He could respond to them in several different ways:

- *Revenge:* He could hand them over to torture, slavery, or execution.
- *Rejection:* He could refuse to sell them grain and send them back to Canaan.
- *Reconciliation:* He could try to repair what is broken.

Reconciliation is the only right plan, but reconciliation requires confrontation—and risk. Sometimes that confrontation is of sin, and that is never an easy road. Confronting is seldom comfortable for either party in that conversation. But true love and true friendship do not placate, excuse, shift blame, rationalize, cover up, or humor sin. True love and friendship confront sin, which is why Proverbs 27:6 says, "Faithful are the wounds of a friend."

> **Reconciliation requires confrontation—and risk.**

Joseph must care enough to confront his brothers. The risk? He knows what these twenty-two years have done in his life, but what have they done to his brothers? God has been at work in his life—what about in theirs? Perhaps he may also have wondered if Benjamin's absence was silent testimony that they had treated him as they had Joseph.

### Joseph's Plan (vv. 9–20)

Joseph's harsh treatment of his brothers would not have been surprising. The ancient historian Herodotus wrote that Egyptians were predisposed to distrust foreigners. As such, Joseph responds to his brothers as an Egyptian ruler would. He lives down to their expectations. Without identifying himself or accusing them of their past actions, he tests his brothers, seeking to discover if God has also been at work in Canaan.

*Joseph accuses them of being spies (v. 9).* In part, spying was what his brothers hated Joseph for when he gave a bad report of them to their father in Genesis 37:2. Now they are forced to look at themselves. Often in Scripture God allows a person's sin to be mirrored back to them in order to produce repentance (as when Nathan confronted David with the parable of the ewe lamb in 2 Samuel 12:1–6).

*Joseph asks for evidence (vv. 14–16).* Joseph basically says, "You claim an honesty that you must be able to prove." This is actually pretty tough. How do you prove an abstract? To underline the danger they are in, Joseph puts them in prison—perhaps the same one he had been in?—for three days. This may seem harsh, but it is a lot better than thirteen years in slavery and prison. And I would suggest that Joseph is not merely getting revenge. I believe that Joseph was buying himself some time to think. What is he going to do with this situation? And again, even more importantly, has God been at work in Canaan? Is the absence of Benjamin evidence that he faced a similar fate to Joseph's and was sold into slavery—or worse? Is reconciliation even possible?

*Joseph announces his faith (vv. 18–20).* Here, Joseph finds a way to answer his questions. After his brothers have been in custody for three days, Joseph's solution begins with what, to the brothers' ears, would have been shocking words: "I fear God." The brothers have made no claim of faith in God, but the ruler of Egypt does! Joseph sees the power and authority of God and declares his fear (awe and reverence) of God. Joseph allows them space to repent and change, and it is a marvelous picture of grace. Humanly speaking, if anyone has the right to revenge, Joseph does—but he deals graciously with those who hurt him. Would you? Would I?

Joseph extends grace—but not without boundaries:

The brothers must leave one brother behind—a form of human collateral.

They may take grain home to their families—caring for their loved ones.

They must bring their other brother with them when they return—to prove their honesty.

Now, how will they respond?

## The Power of Guilt (Genesis 42:21–24)

> Then they said to one another, "Truly we are guilty concerning our brother, because we saw the distress of his soul when he pleaded with us, yet we would not listen; for that reason this distress has happened to us." Reuben answered them, saying, "Did I not tell you, 'Do not sin against the boy'; and you would not listen? Now justice for his blood is required." They did not know, however, that Joseph understood, for there was an interpreter between them. Then he turned away from them and wept. But when he returned to them and spoke to them, he took Simeon from them and bound him before their eyes.

This is one of the most important dialogues in the entire Joseph story. The brothers immediately connect their present misfortune to the event twenty-two years in the past! We see here the awful, destructive power and pressure of unresolved guilt. It has the power to destroy and to erode, and you can never escape it. Its pressure weighs on you perpetually because you carry it with you everywhere you go. For twenty-two years Joseph's brothers have sought to hide the truth of their selling him, but at the first sign of major misfortune, the trouble is immediately seen as some kind of retribution for their actions.

Every family has a sibling who is quick to trumpet "I told you so!" in virtually any situation. In Joseph's family, that person is Reuben. He did in fact warn the brothers about harming Joseph and even intended to sneak back later to rescue Joseph from their hands (37:21–22). Now Reuben reminds them that these consequences are not on him—he warned them.

Joseph understood what they were saying, but they didn't know it. So why did he weep? The text doesn't tell us, but if we use a bit of biblical imagination, there are several options.

- Their conversation provoked memories of his suffering.
- He saw their contrition and felt badly for them in their emotional and spiritual suffering.
- He had been alone for so long that he yearned to reveal himself.

But I prefer another option entirely. Joseph has just heard for the first time of Reuben's attempt to save him. For twenty-two years Joseph had likely imagined that *all* of his brothers (save Benjamin) hated him, but now he knows that at least one brother had attempted to intercede on his behalf. Perhaps there was hope for real reconciliation after all, so Joseph wept.

This is an extremely emotional scene—especially for Joseph. He has heard their confession of guilt. Now he must determine if what he is seeing in them is mere emotional response or genuine repentance. Only real repentance can cleanse our hearts and hands of guilt, otherwise that guilt will consume us.

## Pitiful Selfishness (Genesis 42:25–38)

Then Joseph gave orders to fill their bags with grain, but also to return every man's money in his sack, and to give them provisions for the journey. And that is what was done for them.

> **Only real repentance can cleanse our hearts and hands of guilt, otherwise that guilt will consume us.**

So they loaded their donkeys with their grain and departed from there. But when one of them opened his sack to give his donkey feed at the overnight campsite, he saw his money; and behold, it was in the opening of his sack! So he said to his brothers, "My money has been returned, and look, it is right in my sack!" Then their hearts sank, and they turned trembling to one another, saying, "What is this that God has done to us?"

When they came to their father Jacob in the land of Canaan, they told him everything that had happened to them, saying, "The man, the lord of the land, spoke harshly with us, and took us for spies of the country. But we said to him, 'We are honest men; we are not spies. We are twelve brothers, sons of our father; one is no longer alive, and the youngest is with our father today in the land of Canaan.' But the man, the lord of the land, said to us, 'By this I will know that you are honest men: leave one of your brothers with me and take grain for the famine of your households, and go. But bring your youngest brother to me so that I may know that you are not spies, but honest men. I will give your brother to you, and you may trade in the land.'"

Now it came about, as they were emptying their sacks, that behold, every man's bag of money was in his sack; and when they and their father saw their bags of money, they were afraid. And their father Jacob said to them, "You have deprived me of my sons: Joseph is gone, and Simeon is gone, and now you would take Benjamin; all these things are against me." Then Reuben spoke to his father, saying, "You may put my two sons to death if I do not bring him back to you; put him in my care, and I will return him to you." But Jacob said, "My son shall not go down with you; for his brother is dead, and he alone is left. If harm should happen to him on the journey you are taking, then you will bring my gray hair down to Sheol in sorrow."

After twenty-two years of trying to escape their guilt, God forces the brothers to face it.

*A picture of grace (vv. 25–28).* When you are weighed down with guilt, even acts of kindness are interpreted as threatening. Joseph restores his brothers' money, and they respond with fear, asking, "What is this that God has done to us?" For the first time, they acknowledge God, but it is in terror, not faith. That is what guilt does. It caused them to lie to Jacob so many years before, to hate themselves, and to fear God without trusting Him. One of the most powerful destroyers of relationships is unresolved guilt.

*An explanation of the trip (vv. 29–34).* Once home with Jacob, to the brothers' credit, they tell the truth with no admixture of deception as before (though they still do not confess their past sin and its role in their present circumstances, as they understand it). They explain Simeon's absence and the terrifying discovery of their money in their bags. And they explain that they cannot return to Egypt unless Benjamin accompanies them.

*Jacob's bitterness (vv. 35–38).* At the risk of losing Simeon, the brother left behind in Egypt, Jacob refuses to send Benjamin back with the brothers to buy more grain. Even worse, his words reek of bitter self-centeredness: "Woe is me!" Although he is the least guilty, Reuben intervenes, offering to have his own sons killed if he doesn't bring Simeon and Benjamin back. (How would you like to be Reuben's kids in that moment?) Jacob, however, will not hear of it. He will not let Benjamin leave—perhaps wondering if he might face a fate similar to Joseph's.

So, where are we?

The brothers are weighed down with years of guilt.
Jacob is drowning in self-centered self-pity.
Joseph is confident in God but concerned for family.

How amazing that the one most hurt is the least self-absorbed. He is also the most confident in God and most prepared to reconcile. But there must be confession and repentance from the brothers. It is the only true path to reconciliation and restoration, which may be the heart behind Charlotte Elliott's classic hymn:

> Just as I am, without one plea,
> But that Thy blood was shed for me,
> And that Thou bid'st me come to Thee,
> O Lamb of God, I come! I come!

Just as I am, Thou wilt receive,
Wilt welcome, pardon, cleanse, relieve;
Because Thy promise I believe,
O Lamb of God, I come, I come!

## Questions for Personal Reflection or Group Discussion

1. Consider the contrast between the Joseph his brothers sold into slavery and the leader of Egypt they encountered years later. How does that contrast show God's sovereignty in this story?

2. Are you an "I told you so" person? Why is that comment usually unhelpful in resolving a situation?

3. Imagine the guilt the brothers carried for all those years. Is there an area of your life where you need to confess and repent—first to the Lord, then to the offended person?

4. How did Joseph's actions express grace to those who had hurt him so many years before?

5. How can confidence in God equip you for navigating difficult relationships?

# 8

# A PROCESS FOR RESTORATION

## GENESIS 43

When I was in the tenth grade, I came home from school, flung my books on the table, and started back out the door. My mom stopped me and asked where I was going. "To Scott Wharton's house to play football," I responded.

Her response? "Not until your homework is finished."

"But by then the game will be over!" I countered.

"That doesn't matter," she maintained. "Homework comes first."

So I did what a lot of tenth graders would have done. I snuck out to go play football. As I recall, it was a great game, and we were going to finish in time for me to sneak back into the house before dinner. Then came the last play. I caught a pass and was running for the winning touchdown when I got tackled from behind—into the swing set. When my face hit the swing set, I broke my front tooth. Now I had to go home with undeniable and unmissable evidence of my disobedience.

At dinner, I tried to keep my head down and the damaged incisor out of sight. But unsurprisingly, my parents saw that I was hiding something and demanded I explain my behavior, so I showed them my broken front tooth. In a family with many children and limited finances, this did not go down well. It was the start of a twenty-plus-year dental journey that I could have lived without.

First the dentist tried covering the damaged tooth with a plastic cover, but it kept falling off, so that was changed out. The tooth was pulled and replaced with a partial plate that was intended to be temporary. Eight years later, while a student in college, I was having so much dental pain I was living off Excedrin, so I went to a dentist in the town where I went to school. They took X-rays and announced that they could only give me an estimate—like I had taken a wrecked car to a body shop. I had thirty-six cavities and only thirty-two teeth. So, for the entire summer I spent two afternoons a week being drilled on in a dentist's chair. The problem? The partial plate was almost impossible to thoroughly clean and was holding bacteria against my upper teeth, causing enormous damage.

Flash forward another fifteen years. I was pastoring a church of delightful people in Southern California, and for the first time in my life I had a dental insurance policy. So I went to the dentist, and after the initial exam he said, "You need to get rid of that partial plate. Let me put in a permanent bridge. After all, you have dental insurance, right?"

"Yes," I responded, "but this might be the definition of a preexisting condition."

"Let's write up a proposal," he answered, "and if they approve it, we can do it. If not, you're not out anything."

I agreed, and lo and behold, it was approved! So, the week before Easter, he drilled my remaining front teeth into posts to anchor the bridge. Knowing the bridge wouldn't be ready for a couple of weeks, I asked, "How can I stand up in front of the church on the biggest Sunday of the year with a mouth that looks like this?"

"Don't worry," he said. "We'll put in a temporary one until the real one gets here."

On Easter Sunday, I made it through the morning service and message just fine. But while I was leading the choir's Easter cantata that evening, the temporary bridge came flying out of my mouth! Some of the choir members saw it and started to snicker. Instinctively I caught it in midair and put it in my coat pocket. After the service, I once again had some explaining to do. But at long last the permanent bridge came in and was installed. I thought to myself, *Finally. After over twenty years of dental problems, this is behind me.*

Not so fast.

A month or so after the bridge was installed, I received notice that my dental insurance company had gone bankrupt and I owed the dentist several thousand dollars. It took months and months to pay that off, but indeed it did spell the end of a dental experience that began with a moment of disobedience to my mom when I was fourteen.

The point?

Choices have consequences—and sometimes those consequences have long lifespans. One of the hard lessons of life is that we will perpetually suffer at our own hands if we don't consider the consequences before we make our choices.

> **Choices have consequences—and sometimes those consequences have long lifespans.**

Similarly to me, Joseph's brothers made some devastating choices twenty years earlier, and now those consequences are coming home to roost. Genesis 43 is heavy in repetition to drive home this point, and three vital contrasts continue the story.

## A Character of Deceit (Genesis 43:1–14)

> Now the famine was severe in the land. So it came about, when they had finished eating the grain which they had brought from Egypt, that their father said

113

to them, "Go back, buy us a little food." Judah spoke to him, however, saying, "The man sternly warned us, 'You shall not see my face unless your brother is with you.' If you send our brother with us, we will go down and buy you food. But if you do not send him, we will not go down; for the man said to us, 'You will not see my face unless your brother is with you.'" Then Israel said, "Why did you treat me so badly, by telling the man whether you still had another brother?" But they said, "The man specifically asked about us and our relatives, saying, 'Is your father still alive? Have you another brother?' So we answered his questions. Could we possibly know that he would say, 'Bring your brother down'?" So Judah said to his father Israel, "Send the boy with me and we will arise and go, so that we may live and not die, we as well as you and our little ones. I myself will take responsibility for him! You may demand him back from me. If I do not bring him back to you and present him to you, then you can let me take the blame forever. For if we had not delayed, surely by now we could have returned twice."

Then their father Israel said to them, "If it must be so, then do this: take some of the best products of the land in your bags, and carry down to the man as a gift, a little balsam and a little honey, labdanum resin and myrrh, pistachio nuts and almonds. And take double the money in your hand, and take back in your hand the money that was returned in the opening of your sacks; perhaps it was a mistake. Take your brother also, and arise, return to the man; and may God Almighty grant you compassion in the sight of the man, so that he will release to you your other brother and Benjamin. And as for me, if I am bereaved of my sons, I am bereaved!"

Here Jacob's character is fully exposed in striking contrast to his own sons. It is dishonesty versus honesty. Indeed, Jacob the schemer has spent his whole life as a manipulator and a conniver. He has lived for his own ends and bent the truth however necessary to accomplish them. It seems he has made every choice in life based on what benefited himself. Whether he was lying to Isaac or stealing from Esau, Jacob lived his life based on manipulation instead of faith. The result? Jacob has become a pitiful slave of his own selfishness. The evidence?

When Joseph was taken, Jacob refused to be comforted.
When the famine hit, Jacob looked to Egypt, not God, for rescue.
When Simeon was detained, Jacob failed to see anyone's pain other than his own.

Jacob still hasn't learned. Isn't it tragic that the son of Jacob who turned out the best is the one who was taken away from his influence for twenty-two years? Jacob refused to send Benjamin for Simeon's sake but kept him home for his own sake. Only when they run out of food and his own life is at risk does Jacob send Benjamin along. Notice the dialogue in verses 2–6:

Jacob says, "Go back to Egypt and get more food."
Judah responds, "We can't go because you won't send Benjamin."

Jacob says, "Why did you tell the truth about having another brother?"

Jacob's sons, who have no doubt spent much of their lives lying, stealing, and manipulating like their father, are finally learning to tell the truth—and he rebukes them for it. He hasn't learned anything, but they have. Not only are they learning to be honest; they are learning to be unselfish. Judah puts himself up as collateral for the safety of Benjamin—an expression of self-sacrifice in a family built on self-protection. This is an important first step for Judah, especially when you consider that he led in the decision to sell Joseph all those years ago (37:26–27).

Judah challenges his dad's selfishness by reminding him that he is not the only one who is hungry. Jacob needs to think of his grandchildren, who will also starve unless he releases Benjamin so that they can get more food. Jacob's response is threefold. First, there is a hint of intended manipulation in Jacob's instructions to put together balsam, honey, aromatic resin, myrrh, pistachio nuts, and almonds as a gift (or bribe?) for the man in Egypt. He also tells his sons to take double the money to repay the money that was in their sacks when they returned the first time.

Jacob's second response is lament. His words in verse 14, "May God Almighty grant you compassion in the sight of the man," sound more like empty despair than genuine hope or trust in God.

His third response is soul-crushing self-pity. He hopes the man in Egypt "will release to you your other brother and Benjamin," but he concludes: "As for me, if I am bereaved of my sons, I am bereaved!" (v. 14). He doesn't even name Simeon, who is still in prison in Egypt awaiting their return. His primary concern seems to be his own sense of grief if he loses Benjamin.

To me, Jacob, one of Israel's patriarchs, is one of the most sad and troubling characters in all of the Bible. While God has been working on Joseph's heart and life in Egypt, Jacob has not changed at all from the manipulative schemer who tripped up Esau so many years before. But one question remains: What about the brothers? Have they changed? Judah's offer of self-sacrifice is a hopeful sign, but how can Joseph know for sure the condition of his family after so much time has passed?

## The Confrontation with Joseph (Genesis 43:15–25)

After the contrast between Jacob and his sons comes the second contrast of Genesis 43: guilt versus grace.

> So the men took this gift, and they took double the money in their hand, and Benjamin; then they set out and went down to Egypt, and stood before Joseph.
>
> When Joseph saw Benjamin with them, he said to his house steward, "Bring the men into the house, and slaughter an animal and make preparations; for the men are to dine with me at noon." So the man did as Joseph said, and brought the men to Joseph's house. Now the men were afraid, because they were brought to Joseph's house; and they said, "It is because of the money that was returned in our sacks the first time that we are being brought in, so that he may attack us and overpower us, and take us as slaves with our donkeys." So they approached Joseph's house steward, and spoke to him at the entrance of the house, and said, "Oh, my lord, we indeed came down the first time to buy food, and it happened when we came to the campsite, that we opened our sacks, and behold, each man's money was in the opening of his sack,

our money in full. So we have brought it back in our hand. We have also brought down other money in our hand to buy food; we do not know who put our money in our sacks." But he said, "Peace be to you, do not be afraid. Your God and the God of your father has given you treasure in your sacks; your money was in my possession." Then he brought Simeon out to them. Then the man brought the men into Joseph's house and gave them water, and they washed their feet; and he gave their donkeys feed. So they prepared the gift for Joseph's arrival at noon; for they had heard that they were to eat a meal there.

Joseph invites them to a feast, showing them grace, but they respond with guilt. They are automatically suspicious because they know the guilt in their hearts. As we've seen before, when our hearts are burdened with guilt, even acts of kindness feel threatening.

The response of the steward is amazing. He begins with a powerful Hebrew greeting: "Shalom! Your God, the God of your father, has given you treasure." What an unexpected declaration from a pagan, polytheistic Egyptian! The steward's comment speaks to the influence and impact of Joseph's testimony to those in Egypt over these past years. Simeon is then restored, as Joseph keeps his word. That also had to be something these brothers were unaccustomed to.

Now they are brought to the home of the second-in-command of the most powerful nation on the earth in the midst of a world-wide famine. Still, their guilt is so great that they do not see the honor—only the danger. Again, this is part of the terrible nature of guilt. It turns loose our worst imaginations. As someone wisely said, "My life has been filled with terrible heartaches—most of which never happened!" Guilt feeds fear, and fear paralyzes.

> **While guilt produces fear, grace exposes that guilt so that it can be resolved.**

But, while guilt produces fear, grace exposes that guilt so that it can be resolved.

## A Celebration of Joy (Genesis 43:26–34)

Here we see the third contrast of this chapter: treachery versus tenderness.

> When Joseph came home, they brought into the house to him the gift which was in their hand, and bowed down to the ground before him. Then he asked them about their welfare, and said, "Is your old father well, of whom you spoke? Is he still alive?" And they said, "Your servant our father is well; he is still alive." Then they bowed down again in homage. And as he raised his eyes and saw his brother Benjamin, his mother's son, he said, "Is this your youngest brother, of whom you spoke to me?" Then he said, "May God be gracious to you, my son." Joseph then hurried out, for he was deeply stirred over his brother, and he looked for a place to weep; so he entered his chamber and wept there. Then he washed his face and came out; and he controlled himself and said, "Serve the meal." Then they served him by himself, and Joseph's brothers by themselves, and the Egyptians who ate with him by themselves; because the Egyptians could not eat bread with the Hebrews, for that is

an abomination to the Egyptians. Now they were seated before him, from the firstborn according to his birthright to the youngest according to his youth, and the men looked at one another in astonishment. Then he took portions to them from his own table, but Benjamin's portion was five times as much as any of theirs. So they drank freely with him.

Picture the scene. The brothers bow before Joseph, once again fulfilling his dreams in Genesis 37. Joseph begins by questioning them about the well-being of their father, and they respond. Then his attention turns to Benjamin, his only full brother, and he declares a very un-Egyptian greeting: "God be gracious to you" (v. 29). That greeting not only sounds un-Egyptian; it sounds very New Testament, almost Pauline—not what you'd expect from an Old Testament character.

The experience of seeing Benjamin is too much for Joseph, and he is overwhelmed with joy. It says that "he was deeply stirred over his brother" (v. 30). Literally, the Hebrew says his emotions boiled over. His joy is over a feast of reunion after years of the famine of separation, and Joseph loses it. He runs to his chambers to weep. Imagine what the brothers must have thought at this point!

Upon his return, Joseph "controlled himself" (v. 31) and called for the feast to begin. Woven throughout the feast are clues to his identity, but the brothers do not put it together.

He asks questions about Jacob's well-being.

He doesn't eat with the Egyptians or the brothers (because of his superior position).

His brothers are seated by birth order. How could he know? The brothers are astonished.

He gives Benjamin five times more food than the rest.

120

This is the first of the two final tests in what I am convinced is Joseph's strategy for family reconciliation and restoration. Joseph has to learn two things about his brothers:

Would they be jealous of Benjamin's favored status as they had been of his?

Would they protect Benjamin or abandon him, as they had done to Joseph?

In other words, Have they learned from their mistakes? Joseph must know before he reveals himself to them.

The first test they pass with flying colors. The brothers celebrate though Benjamin is given favored status, receiving five times more than they do. What a contrast is present at this meal: The brothers enjoy a feast; Joseph enjoys his family. They enjoy release from tension; he enjoys reunion with his brothers. They enjoy a moment to forget their guilty consciences; he enjoys the liberty of a clear conscience. For all the evil they brought upon him, he has repaid them with kindness and care.

Genesis 43 has been a series of contrasts—honesty versus dishonesty, guilt versus grace, treachery versus tenderness. But each of these has come about quite simply to reinforce one other contrast:

Joseph has been a slave—but is free through a heart right with God and a clear conscience.

Jacob and the ten brothers have been free—but enslaved to guilt, fear, and lack of faith.

Conflict is as old as the human race, and as we have seen, conflict between brothers is at the root of conflict itself. Cain and Abel, Isaac and Ishmael, Esau and Jacob—brothers in conflict is a reality of our broken world. What does it take to produce reconciliation?

Is "forgive and forget" enough?

Is restitution necessary?

Does love overlook the past, or does real love seek to make the wrongs of the past right?

These are very real issues that all of us face when we deal with our failures—or the failures of others. Joseph shows great love and wisdom as he deals with the need for reconciliation with his brothers, but he does so in an honest way, not a foolish way.

What will it take to set them free? The power of true forgiveness, which we struggle to find apart from God's help and grace to us. As Daniel Webster Whittle wrote, basing his lyrics on 2 Timothy 1:12:

> I know not why God's wondrous grace
> To me He has made known,
> Nor why, unworthy, Christ in love
> Redeemed me for His own.
>
> I know not how this saving faith
> To me He did impart,
> Nor how believing in His Word
> Wrought peace within my heart.
>
> I know not how the Spirit moves,
> Convincing us of sin,
> Revealing Jesus through the Word,
> Creating faith in him.
>
> But "I know whom I have believed,
> and am persuaded that he is able
> to keep that which I've committed
> unto him against that day."

## Questions for Personal Reflection or Group Discussion

1. When have you experienced serious consequences to a choice you made? How was that situation resolved?

2. Have you ever had to work hard at bringing reconciliation to a relationship?

3. When was a time you were shown kindness by someone you hurt? Why is it so hard to show that kindness to someone who has hurt you?

4. As someone who has received God's grace and forgiveness, how can that experience help you to offer grace and forgiveness to others?

5. Only true forgiveness can bring restoration to a broken relationship—whether it is your relationship with God or with another person. Will you pursue that restoration with the help of God's Spirit?

# 9

# A PROCESS FOR RESTORATION CONTINUED

## GENESIS 44

April 4, 1968, was a seminal day in modern American history. On that day, civil rights leader Dr. Martin Luther King Jr. was assassinated in Memphis, Tennessee. As word of the shooting spread around the country, unrest and riots broke out in many major cities. But not in Indianapolis, Indiana. There, Robert F. Kennedy was scheduled to give a campaign speech in his run for the American presidency. The speech had been planned for a predominantly Black neighborhood. Many of his advisers pleaded with him not to go, with the threat of violence weighing heavily on everyone's minds.

But Kennedy went and gave an impromptu speech, even for the first time in public talking about his brother's assassination. The key moment of the speech, however, was when Kennedy dipped back into classical Greek poetry that had brought him such comfort following the assassination of his brother five years before. He quoted from memory from *Agamemnon* by the ancient Greek poet Aeschylus:

Even in our sleep, pain which cannot forget falls drop by drop upon the heart until, in our own despair, against our will, comes wisdom through the awful grace of God.

We have seen Joseph suffer much pain, and as a result he has learned much wisdom. Now, in seeking to reconcile with his brothers, he applies that wisdom in a strategy to restore his broken family.

As seen in the previous chapter, his brothers passed Joseph's first test. They showed no resentment against Benjamin when he was shown favoritism at the banquet. Now comes the second test: Will they abandon Benjamin as they had Joseph, or will they protect him? Joseph puts the second test into place to expose the true condition of their hearts.

## A Prudent Strategy (Genesis 44:1–3)

> Then he commanded his house steward, saying, "Fill the men's sacks with food, as much as they can carry, and put each man's money in the opening of his sack. And put my cup, the silver cup, in the opening of the sack of the youngest, and his money for the grain." And he did as Joseph had told him. As soon as it was light, the men were sent away, they with their donkeys.

After the feast ends, Joseph commands his steward to do several things:

Fill the brothers' sacks with food

Return their money

Put Joseph's silver cup in Benjamin's bag

Why? Because the only way to be certain that the brothers have truly changed is for them to, in a sense, return to the scene of the crime. They must be put into the position of choosing either their own safety, welfare, and benefit or Benjamin's protection, so Joseph creates a situation that will confront them with the choice: rescue or abandonment.

> **The only way to be certain that the brothers have truly changed is for them to, in a sense, return to the scene of the crime.**

Once they are on their way home, Joseph sends his steward and his guards to overtake his brothers, as if they were fleeing fugitives.

### The Brothers' Reactions (Genesis 44:4–13)

> They had just left the city, and were not far away, when Joseph said to his house steward, "Up, follow the men; and when you overtake them, say to them, 'Why have you repaid evil for good? Is this not that from which my lord drinks, and which he indeed uses for divination? You have done wrong in doing this!'"
>
> So he overtook them and spoke these words to them. And they said to him, "Why does my lord say such words as these? Far be it from your servants to do such a thing! Behold, the money which we found in the opening of our sacks we have brought back to you from the land of Canaan. How then could we steal silver or gold from your lord's house? With whomever of your servants it is found, he shall die, and we also shall be my lord's slaves." So he said, "Now let it indeed be according to your

words; he with whom it is found shall be my slave, but the rest of you shall be considered innocent." Then they hurried, each man lowered his sack to the ground, and each man opened his sack. And he searched, beginning with the oldest and ending with the youngest; and the cup was found in Benjamin's sack. Then they tore their clothes in grief, and when each man had loaded his donkey, they returned to the city.

Notice the steward's words of indictment against them:

Why did you return evil for good? (This is the opposite of Joseph, who returned good for evil.)
Why did you steal my master's special divining cup?

The brothers react with shock and dismay—as well as declarations of their innocence. They brought back the money returned to them on their first trip; why would they steal now? They back up their claim with a bold offer: "Kill the guilty and make the rest of us slaves. We are innocent!" The extremity of the offer was no doubt intended to show the absolute sincerity of their hearts.

The steward's reply drives home the point that this game will be played by Joseph's rules, not theirs. "The guilty will be enslaved, but the rest of you will go free." Imagine how the tension mounted as the brothers climbed down from their donkeys. One by one, the steward searches the sacks, from eldest to youngest. This guy has a real flair for the dramatic. He knows exactly where the cup is because he put it there, nevertheless he starts with the oldest and works his way down to Benjamin—letting the tension escalate with every searched bag. Now imagine the brothers' shock and despair as the cup is found in Benjamin's sack! What will they do now?

"Then they tore their clothes" (v. 13). This was an act of grief, mourning, and despair—and the same thing Jacob had done when shown Joseph's bloody coat twenty-two years earlier (37:34). Once again, the brothers have reaped what they sowed. The safest thing for them would be to leave Benjamin in the hands of the guards and go home alive and free—but they don't. No longer do envy and self-interest govern their conduct. At great personal risk, they return to Egypt with their youngest brother. This is tremendously important. Before, they were deaf to Joseph's cries after throwing him into the pit (37:23–25; 42:21). Now, without hesitation, they move to Benjamin's aid, endangering themselves. The evidence is really there—they are changed men.

There are some biblical themes that are continuing spiritual truths that can never be diminished:

The holiness of God

The sinfulness of mankind

The need for repentant faith

And the evidence of repentance in a changed life

The evidence is there. The brothers could easily have escaped with their lives, but they returned at great personal risk out of selfless concern for their brother and for their father.

## Judah's Plea (Genesis 44:14–34)

Notice the brothers' attitude when they return to Joseph's house: "They fell down to the ground before him" (v. 14). They display the humility of men whose pride has been broken. Joseph charges them with the crime, and Judah, the one who led in the decision to sell Joseph into slavery in the first place, steps forward to respond with a powerful speech, given with tremendous eloquence. He appeals to the ruler of Egypt with a series of pleas:

*A plea of guilt (v. 16).* "How can we escape? God has exposed our guilt." The guilt Judah refers to here is not about the cup but about selling Joseph years before and their follow-on deceit of their father. Judah offers no excuses, no rationalizations, no attempts to cover up their sin, and no blame-shifting. He affirms their guilt and submits them all in total to slavery. It is *we*, not just he. Joseph offers the brothers a way out by again saying they can leave Benjamin and return home without him (v. 17), but Judah gives his second plea.

*A plea for mercy (v. 18).* "Please let me beg!" Judah acknowledges Joseph's power in this situation, that he is second only to Pharaoh in all of Egypt, yet he still begs for his mercy.

*A plea for pity (vv. 19–32).* Judah explains their dilemma. He reminds Joseph that he gave them orders to bring Benjamin the next time they came to Egypt to buy food, but their father refused to part with Benjamin. If he doesn't return home now, the grief will kill their father. The phrase "our father's life is so attached to the boy's life" (v. 30) is the same used to describe David's friendship with Jonathan in 1 Samuel 18:1. It shows the depth of Jacob's love for the boy, and Judah shares it without any apparent resentment. Notice in all this speech that Judah's concern and pity is for Jacob and Benjamin, not for himself.

*A plea for a substitute (vv. 33–34).* Judah's final words are shocking: *"Take me instead!"* Again, this is the same Judah who led them in selling Joseph, but he now agrees to slavery in order to free Benjamin. Twenty years before, Judah could care less about Joseph, but now he cares very much—even to the point of taking the lad's place and his punishment with it. Judah's heart has been transformed.

While we have watched God working in Joseph's heart, clearly He has been at work in Judah's heart as well.

Reconciliation is a challenging thing. It is hard work. But it gets easier if we have one component in place—a confidence that God can change hearts. If we genuinely believe God can (and will) work in hearts—including our own—we can move forward in faith with the hope that change is possible.

The alternative? Remember the Hatfield–McCoy feud? It began over a stolen hog, an illicit romance, and long-standing grudges. But the feud was "more than an isolated story of mountain lust and violence between 'hillbillies'—the Hatfield–McCoy feud was a microcosm of the tensions inherent in the nation's rapid industrialization after the Civil War."[1] The result? Between fourteen and twenty people from those two families were murdered during the course of the feud. This is often the consequence when bitterness is allowed to fester. Deaths, jail sentences, and even executions by hanging all flowed from the poisoned stream of the Hatfield–McCoy feud.

> **If we genuinely believe God can (and will) work in hearts—including our own—we can move forward in faith with the hope that change is possible.**

Where might our unresolved bitterness lead? How much better to commit those feelings to a much better and more powerful stream, which William Cowper described this way:

> There is a fountain filled with blood
> Drawn from Immanuel's veins;
> And sinners, plunged beneath that flood,
> Lose all their guilty stains:
> Lose all their guilty stains,

Lose all their guilty stains;
And sinners, plunged beneath that flood,
Lose all their guilty stains.

## Questions for Personal Reflection or Group Discussion

1. Have you ever experienced real bitterness toward another person? Have you been on the receiving end of such bitterness? What was that like?

2. Why is bitterness so destructive? How can repentance, confession, and forgiveness relieve the pressure bitterness creates?

3. Repentance is a change that results in change. How was change evident in the lives of Joseph's brothers?

4. Why is it important that Joseph put his brothers to a series of tests? What benefit did it bring him?

5. Reconciliation is the goal when dealing with broken relationships. Why is reconciliation such hard work?

# 10

# A FAMILY REUNION

## GENESIS 45:1-15

Where I come from, family reunions are sometimes referred to as "family rebellions"—and just so. Reunions can create lots of emotions, tensions, and awkwardness. Broken promises are remembered, imagined grievances are magnified, and long-standing resentments bubble to the surface.

Tension in a family can't be ignored, however; it has to be addressed. And that is what Joseph has been trying to do. In Genesis 44, we saw Judah's great pain at the thought that they were going to lose Benjamin to slavery or worse. But that moment of pain for Judah becomes for Joseph a moment of great joy. It is joyful not because he is inflicting pain on those who hurt him but because the pain of the moment has tested and proven the brothers and the true character of their hearts. Now the time has come for reunion to be experienced and forgiveness to be expressed.

**A Brother Revealed** (Genesis 45:1–3)

Marlene and I enjoy watching a variety of HGTV home makeover shows like *Home Town*, *Fixer to Fabulous*, and *Fixer Upper*.

Each show begins with some decisions about the house and how it can be remade to suit the family's current needs or tastes. Then comes the actual work of remaking the house, which sometimes includes taking down walls, replacing flooring, or even rerouting the plumbing. Once the work is finished, the ultimate moment of the show comes—the reveal. Here the fixers or show hosts give the homeowners a tour of their remade house, revealing all the extensive work that has been done on their behalf. The reveal often is accompanied by tears of joy as the homeowners see their dream home brought to life. It makes for great theater.

In the story of Joseph, this is now the moment for one of the most startling reveals ever. He has twice tested his brothers to see their true character after twenty-two long years of separation, and they have passed the tests. It is time for Joseph to reveal himself to them.

### *Joseph's Tears* (vv. 1–2)

> Then Joseph could not control himself in front of everyone standing before him, and he shouted, "Have everyone leave me!" So there was no one with him when Joseph made himself known to his brothers. Then he wept so loudly that the Egyptians heard it, and the household of Pharaoh heard about it.

Joseph breaks down under the weight of it all. These are now well and truly tears of joy, because the actions and attitudes of his brothers have proven the truthfulness of their words and their hearts. These are also tears of love, because at last (maybe for the first time ever) they can really be brothers.

Joseph clears the room except for his brothers and, as the second most powerful man in the world, sits before them weeping and sobbing uncontrollably—so loudly that he can be heard by the entire household. Even as far away as the household of Pharaoh they can hear him! Imagine what the brothers must be thinking as they watch this tough-minded, powerful man weep.

### The Brothers' Terror (v. 3)

> And Joseph said to his brothers, "I am Joseph! Is my father still alive?" But his brothers could not answer him, for they were terrified in his presence.

This is huge. Finally, Joseph collects himself enough to say a few words, and they are words that shake the brothers to the depths of their souls:

> "I am Joseph!"

Shock waves accompany those few words. The brothers are terrified into silence, for this moment of great joy to Joseph feels like a moment of great threat to them. They had to be stunned; they had told the story of Joseph's death so many times that perhaps they had even come to believe it themselves. Now this once-dead brother sits in a position of power that is terrifying. Their residual guilt creeps out again. What will Joseph do to them?

### A Faith Declared (Genesis 45:4–8)

> Then Joseph said to his brothers, "Please come closer to me." And they came closer. And he said, "I am your brother Joseph, whom you sold to Egypt. Now do not be grieved or angry with yourselves because you sold me here, for God sent me ahead of you to save lives. For the famine has been in the land these two years, and there are still five years in which there will be neither plowing nor harvesting. So God sent me ahead of you to ensure for you a

135

> remnant on the earth, and to keep you alive by a great deliverance. Now, therefore, it was not you who sent me here, but God; and He has made me a father to Pharaoh and lord of all his household, and ruler over all the land of Egypt."

Notice the tenderness with which Joseph approaches his brothers. It speaks of a heart that is overjoyed and longing for reconciliation. What does he say?

*"Come closer" (v. 4).* You can almost see his brothers cringe and back away when Joseph reveals his identity. He draws them back to himself. His actions reveal the love in his heart that longs for relationship. After years of separation, Joseph wants restoration. It's as if he were saying, "We've been apart too long!"

*"Do not be grieved" (v. 5).* "This is a time for joy!" Joseph releases them from their guilt and calls them to join in celebrating this wonderful family reunion.

**Joseph points his brothers to the sovereign God and His divine purposes.**

*"God sent me ahead" (vv. 5–8).* "God was in it! Trust Him as I have." Three times Joseph points his brothers to the sovereign God and His divine purposes (vv. 5, 7, 8). Notice how Joseph presents his circumstances to them.

Verse 5: "God sent me."

Verse 6: "The famine is not over. I'll care for you and your families."

Verse 7: "God was preparing for your rescue."

Verse 8: "See this from heaven's point of view. You were the agents of God's purposes. I am content with that; you should be as well."

Warren Wiersbe wrote of this moment in Joseph's story:

> Joseph's revelation of himself brought his brothers terror, for they fully expected him to judge them for their past sins. But he had seen their repentance; they had bowed before him; and he knew he could forgive them. He explained that five more years of famine would follow, but that he had prepared a place of refuge for them and their families there in Egypt. God had sent him before to save their lives.[1]

Has there ever been a greater, more merciful response to mistreatment and unkindness by a human being than this? I'm reminded of Corrie ten Boom, who told this story following her years in a Nazi concentration camp:

> It was at a church service in Munich that I saw him, the former S.S. man who had stood guard at the shower room door in the processing center at Ravensbruck. He was the first of our actual jailers that I had seen since that time. And suddenly it was all there—the roomful of mocking men, the heaps of clothing, Betsie's pain-blanched face.
>
> He came up to me as the church was emptying, beaming and bowing. "How grateful I am for your message, *Fraulein*," he said. "To think that, as you say, He has washed my sins away!"
>
> His hand was thrust out to shake mine. And I, who had preached so often to the people in Bloemendaal the need to forgive, kept my hand at my side.
>
> Even as the angry, vengeful thoughts boiled

through me, I saw the sin of them. Jesus Christ had died for this man; was I going to ask for more? Lord Jesus, I prayed, forgive me and help me to forgive him.

I tried to smile, I struggled to raise my hand. I could not. I felt nothing, not the slightest spark of warmth or charity. And so again I breathed a silent prayer. Jesus, I cannot forgive him. Give me Your forgiveness.

As I took his hand the most incredible thing happened. From my shoulder along my arm and through my hand a current seemed to pass from me to him, while into my heart sprang a love for this stranger that almost overwhelmed me.

And so I discovered that it is not on our forgiveness any more than on our goodness that the world's healing hinges, but on His. When He tells us to love our enemies, He gives, along with the command, the love itself.[2]

That is love in action and mercy realized. The world's healing hinges on God's goodness, not ours. Through Joseph's story, we have talked about the importance of seeing the hand of God in *all* the circumstances of life. Joseph models a confident trust in a God apparently long forgotten by the nomads of Canaan. This seemingly pagan Egyptian becomes the spiritual mentor for these sons of Israel.

> The world's healing hinges on God's goodness, not ours.

## A Family Restored (Genesis 45:9–15)

"Hurry and go up to my father, and say to him, 'This is what your son Joseph says: "God has made me lord of all Egypt; come down to me, do not delay. For you shall live in the land of Goshen, and you shall be near me, you and your children and your grandchildren, and your flocks and your herds and all that you have. There I will also provide for you, for there are still five years of famine to come, and you and your household and all that you have would be impoverished.'" Behold, your eyes see, and the eyes of my brother Benjamin see, that it is my mouth which is speaking to you. Now you must tell my father of all my splendor in Egypt, and all that you have seen; and you must hurry and bring my father down here." Then he fell on his brother Benjamin's neck and wept, and Benjamin wept on his neck. And he kissed all his brothers and wept on them, and afterward his brothers talked with him.

The reunion, joyous as it is, remains incomplete. The rest of the family must come as well. Here is the conclusion of the matter:

*Gathering the family (v. 9).* "Share the joy! Bring our father down to Egypt as soon as possible."

*A home for Israel (v. 10).* "The land of Goshen awaits you and your families."

*A full provision (v. 11).* "I will care for you. This is why God sent me ahead!"

*God's perfect plan (vv. 12–13).* "Tell our father everything God has done."

*Healing tears, healing talk (vv. 14–15).* "I'm overwhelmed to see Benjamin and talk with all of you again!"

Don't miss the power of this last point. I can't stress this strongly enough. Three powerful verbs punctuate the emotion of the story:

kissed, wept, talked

Compare this to Genesis 37:4, all the way back at the beginning of the story, when the brothers "could not speak to him on friendly terms." Now they sit down and talk. Such is God's sovereign goodness in bringing about a full reconciliation—even better than where they started.

Joseph's forgiveness has resolved the problem of their guilt. In *The Bible Knowledge Commentary*, Allen P. Ross wrote:

> His words form a classic statement on providential control. . . . The certainty that God's will, not man's, is the controlling reality in every event shined through as the basis for reconciliation. No doubt Joseph had consoled himself many times with this principle of faith. He who is spiritual can perceive the hand of God in every event, and therefore is able to forgive those who wrong him.[3]

Another Bible teacher put it this way:

> Joseph displayed his deep faith in the omnipotence of God—overriding Satan, demonic powers, and wicked men to work out His sovereign will and unfrustratable plan. Faith lifted the whole sordid crime out of the pit of misery and self-recrimination and placed it on the mountain peak of divine sovereignty where God's forgiving grace not only heals but wipes away the past and the pain.[4]

That is how powerful God's grace is. It is not really Joseph or his brothers that are in view here but the sovereign Lord and His heart lived out by His servants who trust Him. That is what we see revealed in Joseph's attitude:

A *picture of God's love.* Like his God, Joseph offers his brothers full forgiveness, great grace, and no revenge.

A *picture of spiritual trust.* Charles Swindoll says, "When I'm able, by faith, to see God's plan in my location ['God sent me'; vv. 5, 7], my attitude will be right. . . . When I'm able, by faith, to sense God's hand in my situation ['God has made me'; v. 9], my attitude will be right. . . . When I'm able, by faith, to accept both location and situation as good [50:20], even when there's been evil in the process, my attitude will be right."[5]

That was the key to Joseph's life—he believed in a God big enough to make all things work together for good (Romans 8:28). All through Joseph's story we have witnessed the "all things," and now at last we see the good. The question is, Do we see the good amid the "all things" of our own stories? God is the Shepherd of your heart—trust Him!

Beloved hymnwriter Fanny Crosby penned:

All the way my Savior leads me—
What have I to ask beside?
Can I doubt His tender mercy,
Who through life has been my guide?
Heav'nly peace, divinest comfort,
Here by faith in Him to dwell!
For I know, whate'er befall me,
Jesus doeth all things well;

For I know, whate'er befall me,
Jesus doeth all things well.

All the way my Savior leads me—
Cheers each winding path I tread,
Gives me grace for ev'ry trial,
Feeds me with the living bread.
Though my weary steps may falter
And my soul athirst may be,
Gushing from the rock before me,
Lo! a spring of joy I see;
Gushing from the rock before me,
Lo! A spring of joy I see.

All the way my Savior leads me—
Oh, the fullness of His love!
Perfect rest to me is promised
In my Father's house above.
When my spirit, clothed immortal,
Wings its flight to realms of day,
This my song through endless ages:
Jesus led me all the way;
This my song through endless ages:
Jesus led me all the way.

As Joseph learned to trust the God who led him all the way, so can we. And even in our darkest moments, we can rest in His perfect, unfailing love and wise, good purposes for us.

## Questions for Personal Reflection or Group Discussion

1. Do you enjoy family reunions? Why or why not? What can make them blessed? What can make them difficult?

2. Imagine the brothers' fear when Joseph revealed himself to them. How threatening would that have felt to you if you were one of them?

3. How do God's sovereignty and human responsibility express themselves in this story?

4. When has something very, very difficult in your life turned out to be a great blessing?

5. Why is Joseph's trust in the Lord the key component to the restoration of Jacob's fractured family?

# CONCLUSION

## GENESIS 45:16-28

Joseph and his brothers have been reunited, but there is still work to do. The brothers must now go home and tell Jacob of their past transgression and face his reaction. But at long last, after twenty-two years of separation, the family can be restored and made whole. Joseph and Jacob are finally reunited, and Joseph cares for his family for the rest of his life.

Can you relate to Joseph's story? I know I can. Family relationships are complicated for many of us, and we have to pick and choose which memories to hang on to. I suspect most of us have experienced some level of betrayal or even abandonment, though not to Joseph's extent perhaps. And I'm sure that many of us have experienced broken relationships in our past that we long to see restored or reconciled.

Joseph's story is a very human story because it reminds us on so many different levels how we are broken and how we, as a result, break each other. And when we break each others, those broken relationships are often the hardest things in a hard world.

Our best response is to embrace Joseph's example of living in God's presence and trusting in His good purposes. As we learn to rest in Him, we can find more than just happiness—we can find true peace. As Solomon wisely wrote:

Trust in the LORD with all your heart
And do not lean on your own understanding.
In all your ways acknowledge Him,
And He will make your paths straight.

(Proverbs 3:5–6)

# NOTES

**Chapter 1: A Family in Dysfunction**

1. Homer, *The Odyssey*, trans. E. V. Rieu and Dominic Rieu (New York: Penguin Books, 2003), 11:593–600.
2. "Is My Family Dysfunctional?," Mental Health America, accessed August 19, 2024, https://screening.mhanational.org /content/my-family-dysfunctional/.
3. Richard DeHaan, "Hatred's Bitter Fruit," *Our Daily Bread*, February 18, 1994, go.odb.org/hatreds-bitter-fruit.

**Chapter 2: An Act of Treachery**

1. Stuart W. Sanders, "William R. Terrill (1834–1862)," *Encyclopedia Virginia*, last updated May 3, 2024, https:// encyclopediavirginia.org/entries/terrill-william-r-1834-1862/.
2. John W. Gordon, "Drayton, Percival," *South Carolina Encyclopedia*, last updated July 22, 2022, https://www .scencyclopedia.org/sce/entries/drayton-percival/.
3. William J. Hamilton III, "Brother against Brother at Secessionville," American Battlefield Trust, accessed September 24, 2024, https://www.battlefields.org/learn/articles/brother -against-brother-secessionville.
4. Andrew Bernhardt, "Joseph: A Type of Christ," Andrew Bernhardt's Homepage, May 7, 2012, https://dtjsoft.com/joseph -a-type-of-christ/.

5. "Hatfields and McCoys: American Family Feud," Britannica, August 12, 2024, https://www.britannica.com/topic/Hatfields -and-McCoys.

## Chapter 3: The Life of a Slave

1. Mark Janzen, "What We Know about Slavery in Egypt," TheTorah.com, last updated August 17, 2024, https://www .thetorah.com/article/what-we-know-about-slavery-in-egypt.

## Chapter 4: Betrayed Again

1. G. J. Wenham, "Genesis," in *New Bible Commentary: 21st Century Edition*, ed. by G. J. Wenham, J. A. Motyer, D. A. Carson, and R. T. France (Downers Grove, IL: InterVarsity Press, 1994), 86.

2. Alexander Maclaren, *Expositions of Holy Scripture*, Bible Hub, accessed August 22, 2024, https://biblehub.com/commentaries /maclaren/genesis/39.htm.

## Chapter 5: Forgotten Again

1. Linda Puff, "Forget-Me-Not: A Flower Filled with Symbolism and Lore," Fairfax County Master Gardeners, accessed August 22, 2024, https://fairfaxgardening.org/forget-me-not/.

2. F. B. Meyer, *Joseph: Beloved, Hated, Exalted* (New York: Revell, 1891), 55.

## Chapter 6: Success at Last

1. This paraphrase of James Denney, *The Second Epistle to the Corinthians* (London: Hodder & Stroughton, 1894), 160, is from W. Morgan Patterson and Raymond Bryan Brown, eds., *Professor in the Pulpit* (Nashville: Broadman Press, 1963), 149.

2. Quoted in J. Vernon McGee, *Thru the Bible with J. Vernon McGee: Acts Chapters 15–28* (Nashville: Thomas Nelson, 1991), 159–60.

3. J. Vernon McGee, *Thru the Bible: Genesis–Deuteronomy* (Pasadena, CA: Thru the Bible Radio, 1981), 168.

4. A. W. Tozer, *The Root of the Righteous* (Camp Hill, PA: Christian Publications, 1986), 137.

5. Samuel Rutherford, *Letters of the Rev. Samuel Rutherford* (Edinburgh: Duncan Grant, 1867), 171.

## Chapter 9: A Process for Restoration Continued

1. "The Feud," PBS, September 10, 2019, https://www.pbs.org/wgbh/americanexperience/films/feud/.

## Chapter 10: A Family Reunion

1. Warren Wiersbe, *Wiersbe's Expository Outlines on the Old Testament* (Colorado Springs, CO: Victor Books, 1993), 78.

2. Corrie ten Boom with John Sherill and Elizabeth Sherrill, *The Hiding Place: The Triumphant True Story of Corrie ten Boom* (New York: Random House, 1971) 239.

3. Allen P. Ross, "Genesis," *The Bible Knowledge Commentary: Law*, ed. John F. Walvoord and Roy B. Zuck (Colorado Springs, CO: David C Cook, 2018), n.p.

4. Merrill Unger, *Unger's Commentary on the Old Testament* (Chicago: Moody Press, 1981), 94.

5. Charles Swindoll, *Great Days with the Great Lives: Daily Insight from Great Lives of the Bible* (Nashville: Thomas Nelson, 2005), 34.

# BE STRONG

## IN THE POWER OF GOD

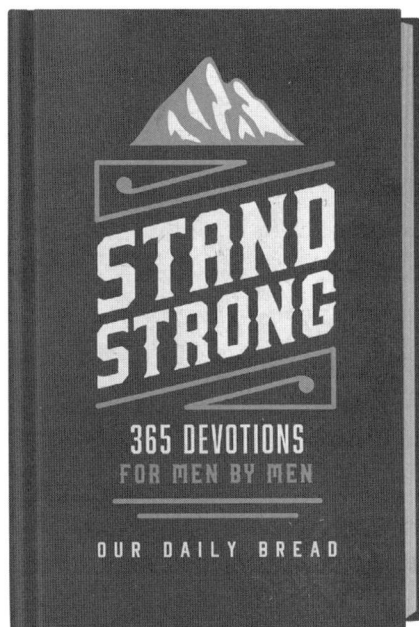

**STAND STRONG**

**365 DEVOTIONS FOR MEN BY MEN**

OUR DAILY BREAD

This collection of personal stories and relevant Scriptures will inspire you to grow in your relationship with God, live a life of integrity, and embrace God's strength in every area of your life.

**Our Daily Bread Publishing®**

## Spread the Word
## by Doing One Thing.

- Give a copy of this book as a gift.

- Share the QR code link via your social media.

- Write a review of this book on your blog, favorite bookseller's website, or at ourdailybreadpublishing.org.

- Recommend this book to your church, small group, or book club.

**Our Daily Bread.**

**Connect with us.** [f] [o]

Our Daily Bread Publishing
PO Box 3566, Grand Rapids, MI 49501, USA
Email: books@odbm.org

# Love God. Love Others.

with 🌾 Our Daily Bread®

Your gift changes lives.

Connect with us. [f] [○]

Our Daily Bread Publishing
PO Box 3566, Grand Rapids, MI 49501, USA
Email: books@odbm.org